ADVANCE P

North Wind Man was a powerful reminder about identity, self-discovery, healing and recovery. It is the journey of a Cree man re-connecting with his Indigenous identity, of overcoming struggles with inner demons, and using his healing path to help others.

For those intent on understanding the ups and downs of the walk to sobriety and healing, this is a must read. It contains words from his ancestors and words from his soul! It takes time to read, and is hard-core humanity revealed throughout! I loved it!

—Mary Anne Caibaiosai, Ojibwe Anishnaabe Artist

In learning about the journey that North Wind Man has travelled, I'm grateful for his willingness to share sacred moments with his mind, body and spirt. He eloquently adds quotes throughout the book that make me feel closer to his stories. The trail from addiction to embracing the honorable gifts that he possesses will inspire many for generations to come. North Wind Man's compelling story is medicine for those seeking a road to reconciliation.

—Myeengun Henry, Former Chief of the Chippewas of the Thames First Nation, Indigenous Knowledge Keeper, University of Waterloo, Traditional medicine and ceremony conductor

Clarence is a helper, visionary, teacher, and brilliant story-teller. Clarence's story of hope and resilience reminds us that to be broken is ordinary. In sharing his very personal journey, we learn the power of community, culture, and connectedness as the foundation of change. An exceptional book written by a beautiful person.

—John Neufeld, Executive Director, House of Friendship

I held *North Wind Man* with reverence for the sacred story held within. I was left with a deep respect for the resilience of Clarence Cachagee and all those who have the bravery to share their own story and sing their own song. I admire Clarence's strength to take the road to find himself. I met Clarence at various turning points along this incredible path and it has been an honour to witness this powerful transformation of intergenerational hurt to wholeness.

It is courageous of Clarence to name the anguish and shame that he endured: in prison, in a broken marriage, in addiction and abandonment. All this to numb the pain of dislocation from the anchor of belonging.

I believe Seth and Clarence have created a book that distills a complex and substantial subject into the particularity of the life of one man who took the journey to find his way home to himself.

Clarence walks with his scars making him an essential helper, healer, speaker and authentic presence in his community. He is a gift for all of us. Clarence who lost himself because of historical trauma has been restored to life and bears witness to the healing and hope that is possible.

This book will be an asset for anyone seeking guidance on their own healing journey and for those of us seeking insight into the indigenous experience in our day.

—Margaret Nally, Spiritual Director, Community Ministry

NORTH WIND MAN

CLARENCE CACHAGEE

SETH RATZLAFF

Cataloguing in Publication
Title: North Wind Man / Clarence Cachagee and Seth Ratzlaff, author.

DDC: 971.004/97
LCC: E78.O5 C33 2022
ISBN: 978-1-990827-03-7

Subjects:
Chapleau Cree First Nation -- Canada -- Biography.
Homeless persons -- Ontario -- Canada -- Biography.
Mennonites -- Ontario -- Canada.
Foster care -- Ontario -- Canada.

region of waterloo

ARTS FUND

Quotations under the heading, "Abby Cachagee (1991)" and chapter 10, "Abby's
Early Years" are taken from the interview with Clarence Hubert Cachagee, and
used with permission from Shingwauk Residential Schools Centre, Algoma
University.

The "Introduction by Clarence" was first published in *The New Quarterly* 150
(Spring 2019), 25-27 and reprinted here with permission.

The identities of some individuals have been concealed for the sake of privacy.

The choices of terminology have taken guidance from several Indigenous style
guides, primarily Gregory Younging, *Elements of Indigenous Style: A Guide for
Writing By and About Indigenous Peoples* (2018).

Gelassenheit Publications
73 Dufferin Street, St Catharines, Ohni:kara, Canada
www.gelassenheitpub.com

For my mother,
Maureen Lindsay

CONTENTS

FOREWORD

Clarence: Wachay! My name is Clarence Cachagee. I also go by another name: Ꮲᐊᐩ Ꮒᐧᐩ ᐃᐩᓂᐅ, which translates into North Wind Man. I'm from the Bear Clan, Fox Lake Reserve, Chapleau Cree First Nation; and I am a beautiful person.

Seth: My name is Seth Ratzlaff. I was born in the Niagara Region to Mennonite parents. My ancestors came from Europe and Russia, and they settled in Canada during the nineteenth and early twentieth century.

Clarence and I met in the summer of 2015 while I was working for The Working Centre, a non-profit organization, downtown Kitchener. My job at the time was coordinator of a second-hand store called Worth a Second Look, called WASL for short.

Clarence: At that time in my life, I was working for House of Friendship as a Shelter-to-Housing Stability Case Worker. That means that I was supporting ten men who had needs. My job was to walk with them, to support them, to do *with* and not *for*, to help them regain some lost life skills and maintain housing stability — which could be very challenging at the best of times. I was in the store looking for a couch for one of the men I was working with. I think he had just recently become housed.

Seth: When Clarence came in one day looking to buy some furniture, he eventually found me. We both felt a connection to one another as we haggled over the price of a couch. (FYI, prices are non-negotiable at WASL.) Before long we started getting to know each other.

Clarence: The funny thing is, when I found my voice back in 2010, I realized that all you have to do is ask a question. If you ask it in the right way, there's almost always room for dialogue/haggling.

Seth and I started a conversation. There was a connection. And I asked, "Why don't you come and shadow me?" Seth was kind of interested in what I was doing. A couple weeks later he came to shadow me for a day, and that's really how our relationship got started. Seth got to see the work I was doing, how I walked with the men in our community.

Seth: I was really impressed with how Clarence worked. He was clearly gifted at supporting people. After that, we started to hang out more often.

As we got to know each other, Clarence shared his life story with me. He told me about his path to becoming a helper, starting with his displacement as a child, his lifelong struggle with shame, and his healing journey, which involved reconnecting with his Indigenous culture. I learned that he was raised in foster care by a Mennonite family, so we had a connection because of my own upbringing and heritage in the Mennonite community.

Clarence: That's when I found out some information about Seth — that he was raised Mennonite and that he had an English degree. And that's when the lightbulb went off — we could come together and make a book happen. In the past I'd done a lot of public speaking and people had encouraged me to share my story and get a book out. I'm not that good of a writer; I'm more of a storyteller. We all have our different gifts. Seth's is to write; mine is to speak.

I offered Seth a Tobacco Tie — which I didn't quite fully explain at the time. It's my understanding that when we need help with something we always acknowledge a person by offering a Tobacco Tie as a way of respecting them and solidifying a partnership. I did explain this in detail after he accepted the Tie.

Seth: When Clarence gave me a Tobacco Tie and asked me to help him write his story, I felt very honoured. As a friend of Clarence, and as someone with a gift to share, I accepted the Tie — not entirely aware of what that meant at the time. The truth is, I really had no idea what I was getting myself into. But a friend had asked me for help, and I was prepared to help as best I could.

One of the first questions that I asked Clarence was why he wanted to write a book and what he wanted it to be about.

Clarence: I wanted the book to be about my healing journey but also about my communities. I think it's important for everybody to feel connected to something. I wanted readers to know that they're never alone, no matter how isolated or far down the rabbit hole they are. There is always hope. I believe that community, culture, and connectedness is the foundation of change.

I also wanted to shed light on the fact that there's positive bundles and negative bundles. I've carried both of those bundles. The negative bundle originated from colonialism, oppression, the Indian Act, the Indian residential school system, and the Sixties Scoop. I had to learn how to carry that bundle to the best of my ability when it was handed down to me from generations before. In time, I was slowly able to learn how to unpack that bundle and then bring in and carry a new bundle full of positive things like love, culture, connectedness, purpose, meaning, ceremony.

Seth: At that time in my life, I was only just beginning to become aware of my identity as a settler in Canada. I wasn't deeply aware of my nation's history in relation to Indigenous Peoples — which had been suspiciously absent from my education — nor was I fully aware of ongoing injustices.

Yet from the beginning, I had a notion that my cultural background was going to pose some challenges for making this book. In Canada (and other settler colonial societies) there is a long history of colonizers and settlers writing about Indigenous Peoples in ways that are insensitive, incorrect, and racist. I didn't want to repeat the mistakes of my ancestors. But at the same time, I didn't want to walk away from the project that a friend had asked me for help with.

After we had both committed to working together, Clarence handed me a big binder full of all sorts of documents — journals, photographs, essays, official records, etc.

Clarence: It was a portfolio that I worked on in college. That portfolio was broken up into seven-year increments of my life. It was a portfolio that we had to put together for an assignment. We had to compile documents and write reflections on them and then present it to our professors.

One thing that blows my mind, regardless of how many times in my life I had lost documents and paperwork, through homelessness, marriage failure, being relocated, I still managed to compile some pretty important and meaningful things that associated me to who I was.

Seth: We started meeting up in the evenings every other week or so. Clarence would host me at his place. After a filling meal — and usually a slice of pie — we'd sit down in his living room and start working. We put together a year-by-year chronology of his life and discussed how to structure the narrative. Clarence gave me a journal entry he wrote in 2014 during a trip from Kitchener to Fox

Lake Reserve. We decided to use the trip as a template for the narrative. We also organized a chronology of important life events according to the organization of his portfolio. In the meantime, I started recording him telling his story.

During my interviews with Clarence, I tried as much as possible to let him tell his story the way he wanted to. I asked open-ended questions and avoided interrupting if I could. If you've ever heard Clarence speak in public, you know that he is a gifted story-teller. I really wanted to preserve that unedited storytelling voice in the book. As we explored writing styles early on, it quickly became clear that it wouldn't work having me edit Clarence's voice in the first-person as a ghostwriter, which felt like a problematic solution to our collaboration. With history in mind, I wanted to avoid manipulating his voice as much as possible and ghostwriting obviously would involve all sorts of invisible manipulation. After experimenting with a few different formats, we ended up using third-person narration, written by me, interspersed with direct quotations from Clarence (which are sometimes lightly edited for clarity with Clarence's consent).

By 2016, we had a large amount of material from transcribed interviews. The book progressed slowly because we were both still working full-time. In the meantime, we also began researching Clarence's past.

Clarence: Through our early conversations, I thought it would be a good idea if we could retrace my steps from withdrawal manage-ment to the treatment centre that I had been to in Waterloo called One-Seventy-Four King. So one morning we met at Park and Glasgow Street. Seth showed up on his bicycle. It was raining.

Then we re-traced my footsteps and had conversations. We talked about what my emotions had been, what I had felt as I had walked that short journey. We talked about what I was thinking about at that time in my life, how I was feeling, reflections on what took me to that decision, what brought me to wanting to go to the treatment centre. Because before that time I had tried numerous times to quit, but it never worked: I had been doing it for all the wrong reasons.

We also talked about what it is like today to reflect on that journey. I think that the whole thing about the journey we were embarking on together is that you can never know where you're going until you know where you're coming from. There are so many layers to who I am and what happened to me, and Seth and I had to go back and peel those layers away. The only place we could start was at the beginning. My journey starts generations ago.

I introduced Seth to my family and my daughters, Carleigh and Madison. In the fall of 2016, we rented a car, left in the wee hours in the morning with my two daughters, and went up to Fox Lake Reserve, Chapleau Cree First Nation. We went to gather more information on my family history and do some interviews. We stayed with my uncle Mike for about four days, visited my aunt, and talked to my cousin Johnny. We went hunting, fishing, and ATVing. And we visited my Métis friends and picked up some bear medicine.

Later, I introduced Seth to some of my foster siblings and my foster mother.

Seth: Clarence introduced me to his family and gave me a list of important people he felt that I should interview for the book. So, as I was interviewing him, I was also conducting interviews with his friends and family in town and up north.

Clarence: In the winter of 2016, I remembered that I had had a conversation with my dad, Clarence (aka Abby), who shared with me that he did a recording back in the early 90s about his time at Shingwauk Indian Residential School. I took it upon myself to send an email to Algoma University and ask if my dad's recordings were there and whether they could be shared with me.

They got back to me and said that they did locate the cassette tapes. They asked me to be patient because they were going to purchase a machine to transfer the tapes to a digital file. A month or two later they sent me three digital files of Abby's story.

It's wild. When I received that email, I didn't want to open those files. It took me a while to even click on it. When I heard his voice, it was just like I remembered it even though he had been gone for over twenty years. It took me a while to go through all those files and to listen to them in depth, because his story is painful. I heard how he was brought up and how he struggled. And I heard how there were parallels in our lives — a lot of those parallels weren't always positive.

Seth: Clarence and I talked about incorporating his father's story into his book by using a transcription of the interviews and decided to include some excerpts from the interviews throughout the book. These are set in italics and are marked with the title: "Abby Cachagee (1991)"[1]

Clarence: Being in the book, I think it honours my dad, his story, his struggles, and his voice. Regardless of the hardships that I experienced in my life, those unanswered 'whys' all make sense now. I want to try to end those intergenerational dysfunctions and start passing on positive bundles.

Seth: In 2017, I went back to school for graduate studies which essentially put the book on hold. When I graduated, we received a timely and generous grant from the Region of Waterloo Arts Fund. I was able to set aside much more time to work on the book.

Clarence: With the grant money secured, we also wanted to go out and spread awareness about the book. We opened a GoFundMe account. We started visiting Mennonite Churches in our region to spread awareness and read excerpts and we were featured in an arts event. Whenever I was facilitating Circles, I also spread awareness and promoted the book.

Seth: The promotion was successful. We had a lot of support from our friends, family, and community. It was very encouraging.

In the summer of 2018, I went up to Sault Ste Marie for the annual Shingwauk Gathering. I was able to spend some time with Clarence's family and learn more about the history of Shingwauk Indian Residential School. I also met some Survivors of the school who generously agreed to read over a draft of a chapter we had been writing that explored Clarence's father's experience in Canada's residential school system.

Clarence: In August 2018, we arranged a three-day trip to North Bay. We stayed in a rustic cottage on Lake Nippissing and arranged visits with my uncles and a cousin from my mom's side of the family. We were doing interviews and gathered more information about family history. I was also able to get some photos of my mom when she was a child. We were able to gain an understanding of how my mom and dad met, and the hardships they faced.

Seth: Over the spring and summer of 2018, we continued to meet and work on the book, including more interviews and revisions.

Graduate studies gave me some useful tools for organizing the interview data we had amassed. I started to use content analysis techniques to pull out important themes in the interviews.

I also began to think much more critically about some of the underlying issues at play in the text as a result of our shared and differing cultural backgrounds. In my position as co-author, I had a lot of power over how the story was told, and this power could easily be misused to turn Clarence's words into something he did not intend. The main way we tried to avoid these potential issues was through our friendship guided by honesty and equality. In practice, this meant we had to start reading the narrative with a critical eye and being open with our feelings and concerns. Did the story say what Clarence wanted to say? Did it say it in the way that he wanted to say it? How would it be interpreted by readers of various backgrounds? What was the apparent message and what was the latent message?

One important issue relates to the power dynamics involved in our partnership. Clarence has a personal story of suffering and resilience which he shares verbally. As a writer, I tried to transpose his story into a written work. That process involves a lot of minor and major decisions. I tried to consult with Clarence as much as possible about decisions, regarding things such as content, structure, and style; but I also had to make a lot of minor decisions throughout the writing. In addition to Clarence's feedback, my decision-making was also guided by ethical considerations.

Some ethical guidance comes from the academic field of social studies. When working with/researching marginalized individuals or communities, Indigenous scholar Eve Tuck warns against the tendency to focus exclusively on the other person/people's damage. Although it might seem sensible to emphasize the suffering of an oppressed people, in order to hold the oppressors accountable, what in fact happens is that marginalized people end up being defined by their suffering. Damage-centred narratives, as a result, overlook the complexity of identities. I took guidance from Tuck in her suggestion that the focus of research should be desire: this approach is "concerned with understanding complexity, contradiction, and the self-determination of lived lives... documenting not only the painful elements of social realities but also the wisdom and hope."[2] Clarence does not shy from disclosing the painful elements of his life; but his story is much more than that. It is also one of resilience and resurgence.

Of course, after all is said and done, I'm aware that my involvement in this project could still be considered a continuation of settler colonialism. Ultimately, I have faith in our relationship, our self-reflection, and in how this book will impact readers. Clarence and I had to be honest and open with each other for this to work. We had to openly share our thoughts and perspectives. If it worked, it was only because we became friends who treated each other as equals.

Clarence: We came at this book through different lenses and then had to work at it as equals. There were stories, events, dates, times, colours; when it all came together, it formed something really beautiful.

Although we say that we are co-authors, there are, in fact, many authors of these real-life events, many different voices. The story depicts the intergenerational traumas that have been passed down from point of contact, through colonization and oppression, through residential schools and the Sixties Scoop, leading up to today.

We both believe sharing these life experiences will benefit individuals and communities across Turtle Island.

This is a narrative about disconnecting and reconnecting with self. It is about the circle of life, the power of trauma harboured and released, the journey from the head to the heart and back, from having a voice, to losing it, and finding it again.

We believe that careful attention to history's injustices and ongoing harm opens future pathways to accountability, healing, and reconciliation.

We believe these truths are relevant to all of us because everyone is on a healing journey, whether acknowledged or not.

Through sharing Clarence's story, we want to inspire communities to work towards unity and equality, working towards right relationships between Indigenous and non-Indigenous Peoples in Canada.

Lastly, in relation to Canada's Truth and Reconciliation Commission's Call to Action Number 22, we believe that our social service systems will be improved with the inclusion of more Indigenous workers and Indigenous healing practices.

The work of building right relationships with our neighbours goes hand in hand with the work of taking care of community members who are marginalized, abandoned, and struggling with substance use and finding safe housing. When you learn how to walk on the land with others as equals, you are at the same time learning how to build (and heal) relationships in the spirit of the treaties our ancestors/nations agreed to.

INTRODUCTION BY CLARENCE

"I think to be a good helper you always have to put the needs of others before your own and be able to step outside of yourself and into their shoes or their situations.[1]

When I wake up, some mornings I pray for understanding, some mornings I pray for compassion; and when I do that, it helps me to be prepared to come out in this community as a helper.

And that's when I do a Smudge. When I smudge, I burn sage and medicines. In the mornings I take time and I think about the teachings.

I smudge my hands so that the smoke of the medicines will cleanse my hands so that anything I touch or create, I'll touch and create it in a good way. And if that means touching someone physically, mentally, spiritually, or emotionally, or if that means filling out paperwork, or if that means holding a door open for somebody, or if that means maybe just shaking somebody's hand, I will do it.

And then I cleanse my eyes with the smoke so that my eyes are clear, so that when I see things throughout the day, I can see them in a good way, in a kind way. And it's funny because sometimes when I see people coming and I know they want to talk to me, I might question their motive, or I might say, "Oh geez, here they come again." But I catch myself because I can remember being in that situation; and I remember the importance of being able to have that person or those persons that I could go to no matter how bad my day was, that they would accept me and listen to me. So that's why I cleanse my eyes, so that I can see that and be aware of that.

I cleanse my ears, let the smoke wash over my ears so that when I hear things, I hear them in a good way. And I don't know how many times when I've been helping people and they're talking to me and I hear these stories, I either put something together in my own mind or I'm questioning their motive — or I'm hearing myself in the stories they're telling me. So, cleansing my ears gives me some understanding.

And then I'll take the smoke when I'm smudging and I'll wash it over the top of my head so that when I have thoughts, I'll have good thoughts, I'll have pure thoughts, I'll have kind thoughts. And that really comes in handy when I'm serving the people in Creation because patience and understanding and acceptance is a big tool that I use when I support these individuals — because I don't know the whole story, but I usually know that there's something deeper going on that stems from why we need to talk about situations.

And then I take the smoke and I bring it up to my throat. I cleanse my throat so that when I speak, I have a strong voice and so that when I speak, I say kind words, because I don't know how many times I've had to bite my tongue because I know that words can cut. And once you say something you cannot take it back. Bones can be broken but words can cut like a knife. So that's why, when I speak, I have to make sure that I'm saying the right words, that I'm applying the right words, the appropriate words to the individuals that I'm supporting or walking with.

And then when I smudge, I bring the smoke to my heart so I have empathy and so I have love for myself, and I have love for others. And that empathy I think goes a long way in the work that I do. It's not sympathy but it's empathy. I can empathize. But I'm very guarded with my heart too, though. So hopefully smudging my heart daily will soften it up and it'll make me not only love myself, but it will make me love others.

And then I bring the smoke into the core, into my centre, so that I can stay centred. I don't really bring it in so that I can stay balanced because if I seek balance and if I don't attain it, then I could become frustrated. So I just try to stay centred, centred within my mind, body, spirit, and emotions, because out of those four quadrants, I'm in the centre along with the Creator.

And then I smudge down my legs, smudge down each leg so that when I walk out in this community I can stay centred, I can stay grounded, and I can remember that each step is sacred as I walk along Mother Earth. And along with that sacredness comes the teaching that each and every one of us is sacred and equal within the circle of life. And then I usually smudge up to the air that I breathe, and I smudge down to the ground that I walk on.

And those practices, those ceremonies, those motions that I go through every morning help me to be all I can be as a helper.

And then I pray. I pray for the ones who are lost. I pray for the ones who are broken. I pray for the ones who are taking their last breaths. I pray for the ones who are caught in the grips of addiction. I pray for the ones who are grieving. I acknowledge and ask for forgiveness for all the ones I have wronged, all the ones that I have hurt, all the ones that I did unjust things to. And then I also acknowledge and pray for all the ones who have helped me, all the ones that have been there for me, all the ones that have walked with me, all the ones who have supported me, all the ones who have never given up on me, because those are the ones that I think really influenced me to do the work that I do today.

I always wanted to be a helper. I always knew that I was good with people. People used to say, "Clarence, man, you're good with children. You work really good with children." But I just, I'm not at that stage yet; I don't know if I'll ever be at that stage where I can work specifically with children. I really enjoy working with men. But I knew the only way that I could become a helper is that I had to first help myself. I knew I had to practice what I preached.

But I really enjoy doing the work that I do. I have my bad days. I can see sometimes where judgment washes into my thoughts. Sometimes I question the motives of the men I work with. Sometimes I stereotype them. But it's only for a split second and then I catch my judgmental thoughts. When I do, I can always — usually — divert them, or come back to the sacredness of life, how everybody is a sacred part of Creation, and how it's ordinary to be broken.

1

PURPOSE, MEANING AND DIRECTION

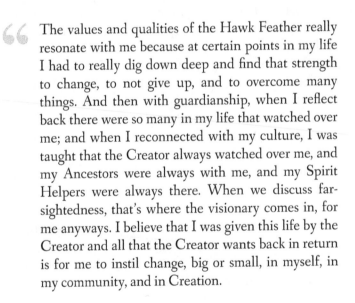 The values and qualities of the Hawk Feather really resonate with me because at certain points in my life I had to really dig down deep and find that strength to change, to not give up, and to overcome many things. And then with guardianship, when I reflect back there were so many in my life that watched over me; and when I reconnected with my culture, I was taught that the Creator always watched over me, and my Ancestors were always with me, and my Spirit Helpers were always there. When we discuss far-sightedness, that's where the visionary comes in, for me anyways. I believe that I was given this life by the Creator and all that the Creator wants back in return is for me to instil change, big or small, in myself, in my community, and in Creation.

Early one humid morning in August, 2014, Clarence Cachagee waited for a bus at Charles Street Terminal in downtown Kitchener, Ontario. Beside him on the bench was his red knapsack. Around him was a mild smell of cologne and the bustle of morning commuters: students lodging in Kitchener on their way to the universities and colleges in the neighbouring city of Waterloo; workers catching an early bus to the outskirts of town where the few remaining factories still operate; or maybe they were on their way to retail jobs in the department malls at the end of the transit lines. In slacks and a t-shirt, Clarence took in his surroundings.

Not too long ago he lived in an apartment only a block away on Gaukel Street, a subsidized housing unit. Just across the street was Victoria Park, an expansive green space in the heart of the city with a small lake that Clarence visited when he needed to process difficult times. He was waiting for a Greyhound bus to Toronto; from there he intended to transfer to a bus heading north, which would take him all the way to Sault Ste Marie, a small city on the north shore of Lake Superior, about ten hours by bus from Toronto. Once in Sault Ste Marie, he planned to meet up with his cousin who was going to drive him two hours further north to Fox Lake Reserve, Chapleau Cree First Nation. Clarence recalls his thoughts as he waited for the bus:

> I guess I was going there for some closure, for maybe some direction. I think I was also going there to see if there were some opportunities. I had just finished schooling and I was thinking about moving up north to work with my brothers and sisters there.

It will be a long journey. It has been a long journey to this terminal. With its vandalized benches and sun-bleached shelters, this used to be a good place to hunker down and warm up in the winters, especially Sunday mornings after spending the night half-sleeping on a foam mattress in a stale church gymnasium, surrounded by snoring bodies and pungent feet. Just across the road on the other side of the platform was a cement wall that, not too long ago, Clarence had slouched against, too drunk to go on, as his friends had boarded a bus, oblivious to their incapacitated companion. When speaking of alcohol use, Clarence emphasizes:

> I want the listener to always remember that it's not necessarily that I had a drinking and using problem. I had a living problem, and drugs and alcohol helped me cope with life.

In spite of his past, Clarence's body remains strong. He has a deep chest and thick arms with defined veins, a solid build. His skin is healthy, hinting at copper in the summer sun. His hair is buzzed and his face clean-shaven.

CLARENCE WAS BORN in September 1965 in the city of Kitchener, Ontario, to Maureen Lana (Lindsay) and Clarence Hubert Cachagee. To avoid confusion, young Clarence soon went by his middle-name, Michael. Both of his parents were going through tough times back then. Two years earlier, only sixteen years old, Maureen had given birth to Clarence's sister, Cheryl. Maureen had grown up with her blue-collar family of Scottish and Irish descent, near North Bay, Ontario. Clarence's father, who went by the name Abby, was a member of Chapleau Cree First Nation. Only months prior to meeting Maureen, he had been released from Canada's residential school system, in which he had spent most of his upbringing.

Clarence was born to parents who were both survivors, each in their own way. Maureen's parents struggled with alcohol use and were unable to provide a safe housing environment during her upbringing. Abby was placed in the care of the child welfare

3

system just before he turned three years old and then transferred to an Indian Residential School when he was six. Before Clarence turned two, he and his four-year-old sister were taken in by Children's Aid Society of Waterloo Township and eventually placed into permanent foster care with a Mennonite farming family in New Dundee, a small town on the outskirts of Kitchener. As he grew older, he became troubled by the 'whys' – all the unanswered questions of his circumstance and he started running away from his foster home, seeking answers which lay beyond his grasp.

When Clarence grew up, he and his high school sweetheart started a family. They married, purchased a home in the suburbs of Waterloo, and raised two daughters. From the outside, it looked as if all was well full-time work, two children, and a happy couple. But in time, the facade of a functioning, middle-class family started to disintegrate, at first piece by piece, little by little, and then turning abruptly into a cascade of dysfunction. As Clarence recalls:

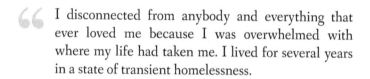

> I disconnected from anybody and everything that ever loved me because I was overwhelmed with where my life had taken me. I lived for several years in a state of transient homelessness.

It has been quite the journey from those tumultuous days to this bus terminal in Kitchener. At forty-nine years old, Clarence was about to begin another chapter in the story that he used to try so desperately to forget, in whatever way he could. But this was to be a different kind of chapter, a new kind of story. He laid some loose leaf tobacco on the ground. He explains:

> Semah (tobacco), when we pray with it and as soon as it touches the ground, it opens a direct or immediate channel from this world to the next. So that takes our prayers up to the Creator. I was asking for safe travels for myself and everyone else who would be traveling.

I had teachings to always pray forward and remember others if and when we pray for ourselves. There are always those behind praying for us.

Waiting for the bus at the Charles Street Terminal, Clarence was in the Grand River Valley, on the traditional territory of the Attawandaron (Neutral), Anishinaabe, and Haudenosaunee Peoples. Clarence remembered a conversation he had a couple years ago with an important mentor, Donna Dubie. She was the first to tell him about the history of this land, its original inhabitants, and how his own life circumstances intertwined with them.

BEFORE THE MID-SEVENTEENTH CENTURY, Attawandaron First Nations were living on the land between Lake Huron and Lake Ontario. Attawandaron translates "peoples of a slightly different language,"[1] meaning that this is the name used for them by neighbouring First Nations. In the seventeenth century, the Attawandaron encountered English traders who began to call them the Neutral people, because they were situated between two conflicting nations: the Huron Nation to their north and the Haudenosaunee Confederacy to their east.

The Haudenosaunee — meaning those who make the longhouse together — are a confederacy of First Nations that traces its origin to nearly one thousand years ago.[2] At that time a Huron individual known as the Peacemaker journeyed across Lake Ontario in a canoe made of white stone. With the assistance of two helpers, he then managed to unite long-conflicting nations under the Great Law of Peace. Originally five Nations — the Mohawk, Oneida, Onondaga, Cayuga, and Seneca — the Tuscarora Nation joined later, making the Six Nations. The traditional territory of the Six Nations reached from the Niagara River in the west to the Atlantic Ocean in the east.

In the seventeenth century, the area now referred to as

southern Ontario was commonly known as The Beaver Hunting Grounds. At that time, First Nations populations in the area were suffering major population decline due to epidemics of new European diseases. Adults were most susceptible to death, and as the Haudenosaunee people's adult population dwindled, and with them the skills and expertise needed to sustain the community, their society became more dependent on European trade goods for survival. In return, European traders, who especially desired fur pelts, gained access to hunting territories that were increasingly important for the survival of Indigenous Peoples.

In the 1650s, the Haudenosaunee, grieving the losses caused by deadly diseases and more reliant than ever on the fur trade economy, moved into the Beaver Hunting Grounds, competing with the Attawandaron for control of the territory. In some cases, this led to clashes and eventually the dispersal of the Attawandaron; however, the Haudenosaunee were also desirous of rebuilding their society, and many Attawandaron refugees or captives were adopted into Haudenosaunee communities — mainly through the Seneca Nation.[3] Soon enough Haudenosaunee longhouses appeared on the north shore of Lake Ontario.

Then, in the late seventeenth century, the land was further contested and taken control of by Anishinaabe from the north, known as the Mississaugas. However, in 1701, the Mississauga and the Haudenosaunee Nations made peace with one another, forming a treaty that provided a basis for sharing resources and jurisdiction of the land. The agreement was captured symbolically in the Dish with One Spoon Wampum Belt. The symbols of this Wampum Belt set the terms for shared responsibility and use of the land while preserving the sovereignty of the two nations.[4] The dish pictured in the Belt represents the land with all of its gifts and resources, and the symbol of one spoon sustains all the people living on the land; each member should only take from the land as much as needed for survival, and it is everyone's responsibility to ensure that there is enough for all — to ensure that the common dish remains bountiful. The British Crown also made treaties with the two nations, agreeing to abide by the principles of the One Dish Treaty, and promising to help protect the Beaver Hunting Grounds from foreign aggression.

As European colonization of the land intensified during the eighteenth century, European settlers more frequently stole Indigenous Peoples' lands. In 1763, partly in response to this illegal encroachment, the English King issued a Royal Proclamation that outlawed the private purchase of Indigenous lands. From that point on, according to British law, only the Crown could purchase land from Indigenous Peoples in a public gathering.

When the thirteen American colonies rebelled against British rule and the American Revolutionary War began, the British petitioned both the Mississauga Nation and the Haudenosaunee Confederacy for military assistance. Mississauga warriors aided the British in the war. However, initially, the Confederacy was reluctant to involve itself in what it saw as a family dispute, but eventually most Haudenosaunee nations allied with the British against the American revolutionaries.

The war ended with British defeat, and during the post-war negotiations, the British ceded Haudenosaunee territory to the Americans without compensating the Haudenosaunee for their allegiance. Many Haudenosaunee removed to Fort Niagara, establishing camps there, requesting that the British government hold up its end of the deal. Eventually, Sir Frederick Haldimand, in an effort to make up for British negligence, made compensation to the Haudenosaunee by purchasing from the Mississaugas the land ten kilometres on either side of the Grand River from its source to its end. This large swath of land, known as the Haldimand Tract, "which them & their Posterity are to enjoy for ever" was then granted to the Six Nations.[5]

Clarence had risen early that August morning, a habit of his for as long as he could remember. Knapsack in hand, he boarded the first inter-city bus heading to Toronto. No one sat in the seat adjacent to him, and he was content with the solitude. The ride ahead would be a long one, and he intended to journal his reflections in the meantime. It would be at least sixteen hours on the bus, and then another two hours in the car to Fox Lake Reserve, Chapleau Cree First Nation.

When the coach bus lurched out of the station Clarence let out a sigh. Despite all that has happened so recently, he still had a lot of work ahead of him, *the hardest work*: mending wounds, breaking old habits of thought and action, healing broken relationships — as well as working through all the surprises that would surely come up along the way. Reflecting on that pivotal time in his life, Clarence summarizes:

> I was rebuilding relationships with my children, rebuilding relationships with my community. I was finding purpose, meaning, and direction.

The bus turned onto Joseph Street, then onto Victoria Street where it headed east and crossed the Highway 7 bridge over the Grand River. The first stop would be in Guelph, before taking the expressway to Toronto, where Clarence planned to catch his layover and head north. He watched through the window as the city slid by, much like a good portion of his life had — muted.

2

EARLY YEARS

66 My story doesn't start with me, it starts with my parents, and it starts generations before them. To the best of my understanding, my parents were two young people coming from broken families, trying to find something they never had: a loving relationship. My dad, Abby, came from a broken family. My mom, Maureen, came from a broken story. Today I have an understanding that to be broken is to be ordinary but back then there was nothing ordinary about it. Cheryl and I were taken into foster care in 1967, and eventually we ended up with the Reiers, who raised us.

It was Eileen Reier's youngest daughter, Margaret, who originally suggested to her mom that perhaps, now that three of Margaret's five siblings had moved out, it might be a good idea to open the household for foster care. The idea appealed to Eileen, and soon enough she was talking with friends from church who had themselves been providing foster care through the child welfare system. Margaret explains how it started: "They had an empty house and mom had some time. This is what she wanted to do with her extra time: get a couple kids and look after them... The kids would come and stay for a little while until they found permanent adoptive homes. And that's sort of what we thought we were getting into."[1] One thing led to the next, and after making the arrangements with the Children's Aid Society (CAS), in 1966, Eileen and her husband Ken were preparing their home for a new addition. Little did they know that they would be getting two.

The Reiers were a Mennonite family who ran a pig farm in New Dundee, Ontario, a small town twenty minutes southwest of Kitchener. They lived in a modest, two-storey farmhouse, with white siding and a back porch. There were two barns on the property, to farrow and finish nearly three hundred pigs. The farm included eighty acres of land, of which about fifty was pasture, the remaining was a woodlot situated at the back of the property. Meandering across the fields and into the forest was a small stream; Ken had dug out a pond for swimming near where it disappeared into the woods. "My dad was always very, very gentle," Margaret says, "a person of few words. He just didn't talk a lot." She goes on: "I remember we used to say, 'Mom, he never says anything, and he never tells us anything.' She would always say, 'Well your dad really loves you. He just can't express himself.' " Eileen was a strong-willed woman. "It was my mom who really directed things," Margaret explains. "I think she made a lot of the decisions."

Several years before Clarence and Cheryl arrived, the Reiers' barn had burnt down. It was Eileen who convinced Ken that they start a pig operation in its place. And she did a good portion of the planning and research to make it happen.[2]

The farmhouse was in the middle of renovations in November 1967 when CAS asked them to provide temporary care for two young siblings. The Reiers agreed. Clarence had recently turned two and Cheryl was four when they arrived. Of the Reiers' five children, only Keith and Margaret were still living at the house. Keith — the youngest son, seventeen at the time of their arrival — was upgrading the old home's plumbing and electrical wiring. Margaret, who was twelve then, recalls when Clarence (known as

Mike) and Cheryl first arrived, "we had been told that they had been in at least six different homes by the time they arrived at our place... He didn't talk a lot when he first came. He had a speech impediment; his sister Cheryl would have to interpret for him."

Clarence says:

> As far back as I can remember, the only thing that was constant in my life was change and my sister Cheryl. I thank the Creator that we were never separated and am forever grateful that we are siblings.

Having his sister there with him during those early years of displacement was a major source of support for Clarence, her love an anchor during stormy times.

One of the first words that Clarence started to say in his new home was an unexpected one. His sister clarified for everyone: he was calling his new mother "Teacher." Eileen didn't think much of it. She was prepared to take care of these children no matter what they called her. Keith thinks that Clarence continued to say that for a few months before switching to "mother."

"They were really energetic. They were neat kids," says Margaret. Clarence quickly developed a reputation for being a mischief-maker. He was both curious and outgoing. When friends and family came to visit, he would literally crawl on them, pulling at their ears and grabbing their hair, becoming fully acquainted with new people in his childlike way. Margaret also remembers a highly empathetic child, one that was keenly aware when others felt pain — she recalls that he would always remain close to anyone who appeared to be suffering.

As the foster placement was meant to be temporary, Clarence and Cheryl appeared in the local newspaper under Today's Child, a weekly column that CAS used to advertise children for adoptive homes. The column often made the children it featured feel disposable and unwanted; and it often used insensitive language to describe them.

Clarence and Cheryl in Today's Child *column*

Clarence still has a copy of the newspaper clipping and looking at it now, he reflects:

> It was kind of hard, you know, when, even today, when I see those pictures because you see these two young children, three and five years old, and they're smiling in the picture in the newspaper, but really these children are broken. They're lost and there's so much confusion and so many unanswered questions.

He recalls an early memory from that time period: a trip to

Waterloo Park with social workers. He and Cheryl were dressed in nice new clothes and taken to the small zoo in the park, where a social worker took pictures of them standing in front of the animals.

> I just remember at Children's Aid, I always felt like I was an object. I always felt like I was a thing and not a person — you know what I mean? — because it was almost like we were auctioned off. Or, we really didn't have parents, so we were always put over here, we were put over there, but then we were bought back.

In March 1968, CAS found Clarence and Cheryl a prospective home for adoption and took the two from the Reiers for a visit. They were in this home until November, at which point the placement broke down. Clarence and his sister were then returned to the care of the Reiers. Soon after, CAS found a second home. Again, this placement didn't work out, lasting no longer than a couple of weeks.

Margaret remembers when Clarence and Cheryl came back to their home the second time: "I got the job of telling Keith that they were coming back. I've never seen him look so happy." Keith describes why he thinks they were at the adoptive home for so short a time: "They were at our place long enough to know that they didn't want to leave, and they created havoc for the people who wanted to adopt them."[3]

At this point, Ken and Eileen realized that the two children they brought into their home for temporary care might not be so temporary after all. Clarence and Cheryl were starting to become part of the family. To complicate the matter, the Reiers also discovered that CAS was preparing to split up the brother and sister in order to find them permanent adoptive homes — a practice that was alarmingly common for Indigenous siblings in the welfare system. With a growing affection for the two children, the Reiers began to consider raising them as part of their family. The only problem was that they didn't think they would be able to handle the burden of the financial cost. However, in response to their concern, CAS offered the Reiers a new arrangement: the organization would no longer seek an adoptive home for the children, and it would continue to provide an allowance so that the Reiers could afford to take care of them. The Reiers agreed.

So it happened that Clarence Michael and Cheryl Cachagee were taken into permanent foster care by a Mennonite family in a town called New Dundee, part of the Regional Municipality of Waterloo, situated within Block Number Two of the Haldimand Tract, on the traditional territory of the Attawandaron, Anishinaabe, and Haudenosaunee Peoples.

Soon after Eileen and Ken decided to raise them, the two foster children started settling in as best they could. The farm, with its forests, fields, gardens, and pond, became home to them, and the Reiers became family. Clarence grew close to his foster siblings, Margaret and Keith. Margaret admits she used to dress up Clarence as if he were her sister — she says he went along with the game quite happily. Keith had grown quite fond of him too, often playing the role of prankster older brother.

> I was grateful and I am grateful for what they did for me, how they accepted me and gave me a place to stay where all my needs were met. Growing up, they taught me how to skate; they taught me how to live; they taught me how to be a child.

When Clarence was young, he struggled with asthma and eczema. His asthma attacks usually happened at night. During the worst of them, Eileen would stay up holding him, helping him manage to catch moments of sleep in between stuttering breaths. When the attacks were especially bad, the family had to take him to the hospital where he was put into an oxygen chamber. "And as soon as he was feeling well enough," Margaret recalls, "he'd be running up and down the halls creating trouble, embarrassing my mother." Indeed, most reports of Clarence at this age describe a child bursting with energy, one who was difficult to contain indoors; as a result, he was often sent outside to play. Running in the fields, exploring the woods, swimming in the pond, Clarence learned how to lose himself to the wonders of the world.

Clarence and Cheryl dressed as each other, posing with Eileen

I think at a young age I knew I was connected. I'd find comfort in Mother Earth. There was always a connection there, where I felt at home. I can remember when I was young, I would explore, playing in the woods, digging; it would captivate me for hours.

Clarence holding a frog, 1971

The Reiers often found him playing in the vegetable garden, digging up curled grubs and thick earthworms. One spring day after a heavy rainfall, Clarence went out to the garden wearing his oversized Wellington boots. Stomping in the thick mud, he managed to get himself stuck; the more he struggled, the deeper his boots sank. The Reiers came outside when they heard him yelling and found the little boy sobbing and immobilized in the garden, his small rubber boots almost buried in the mud. The story is a family legend.

Despite the reports of his foster siblings, Clarence also feels that he was a very shy child, especially at school.

> I do remember Kindergarten. I remember I was always, always the shy kid. I was very insecure. Maybe that was because I couldn't talk right; I had a speech impediment. Maybe that brought me some shame or some guilt at a young age.

As he became more aware of his surroundings, he stopped displaying that innocent curiosity around strangers. Clarence remembers how, as he grew older, he started to feel awkward and keep to the background when visitors came to their house.

> I just remember I didn't feel good growing up. Sometimes I just felt out of place. It was hard to find a place to fit in, or to know where I fit in... I knew that I didn't belong to that family, that cell, that network of people.

By 1972, when Clarence was seven years old and in grade two, he had outgrown his speech impediment but was still insecure at school. Learning to read and write was proving difficult, and he was struggling to make new friends. At the end of the school year, due to his poor marks, the school administration decided to hold him back from the next grade.

> I think my first experience with failure was when I was seven years old. All those friends that I made through those few early years, I lost them because they held me back. I remember how devastating that was, internally, watching those people move forward, knowing that they were

going into grade three and knowing that I wasn't
going.

After this, Clarence became angrier at school. Other children
would sometimes make fun of him for his learning challenges. He
started getting into fights. One time, when his classmates didn't let
him join in a game of baseball, he grabbed a bat and swung it into
the groin of another student. By grade three, he had been
suspended at least once.

Clarence was beginning to think about himself as an outcast,
an ill-fitting piece to the puzzle of his school and family life. He
started hanging out with two other boys who also had a kind of
outsider status. The Reiers were not impressed with his new
friends.

> I became a bully because I wanted some of those chil-
> dren in school to experience the pain that I was expe-
> riencing... I'm not happy that I did that, but that's
> where I was at that time in my life, and when I pray
> today, I ask for forgiveness, for the wrongs that I have
> done, and those children are always in my prayers.

Every day after school, Clarence and his sister Cheryl were
dropped off by the bus at the rural route that led to the Reiers'
farm. It was a short walk home, but they usually took their time.
There were ditches and creeks to explore, and school gossip to
discuss. Not surprisingly, sometimes they found trouble too.

In 1972, along their walk home there was a construction site,
the new cement bridge over Alder Creek. Clarence recalls one of
those days:

> They had a whole bunch of tires along the side of the
> bridge, for whatever they were doing. Cheryl and I
> threw them all overboard into the creek. Then some-

body found out, and Cheryl and I had to go get the tires out.

Clarence remembers helping his sister pull the tires out of the creek, however she reports a different story. According to her memory, Clarence didn't want to do the dirty work and let her stomp through the mud while he stayed at the water's edge. Apparently, he had spotted a crayfish under a rock and didn't want his toes pinched.

But as he grew older and stronger, he did start to help out on the farm. The Reiers made a mask for him so that his asthma wouldn't be aggravated by the dust in the barn.

> I would always help with the chores, as much as I could... I never got hurt at all. Dad would always show me what would happen. He'd show me the repercussions. He'd tell me about the gas in the silos and manure tanks. He'd show me what augers could do.

Life on the farm might mean tedious work, such as helping to pick out rocks in the field, as Eileen drove the tractor ahead pulling a large cart for the stone collection (a job no one enjoyed). But the children had fun too. The woods were always a world waiting to be discovered. And Clarence and his sister both loved to swim in the pond. Clarence remembers one swim in particular when Cheryl brought a friend over. All was well in the pond until Cheryl's friend let out a piercing scream: she had discovered a couple of leeches clinging to her leg. Clarence describes what happened next:

> Our mom Eileen came out to see what all the commotion was, assessed the situation, and went back inside to get some salt.

Clarence was sometimes mischievious too, for example, one evening when Eileen sent him out to retrieve Ken from the fields.

> The back field — the back flats we called them — were behind the farm. We had a pond and a laneway back there. I saw a skunk running around. It started running away so I took off after it, of course. In full flight I gave it a good hoof.

Kicking skunks is a good way to learn a valuable lesson: animals have feelings too. Clarence came running back to the house crying and reeking of that distinct, sour smell of skunk. Eileen made him strip off his clothes outside, threw the garments into the garbage, and sent him to the bathtub for a soak in tomato juice.

Although he was certainly getting used to living with the Reiers, Clarence had not totally forgotten his displaced roots. Vague memories hinted at a life before this one. Even today, he can still recall one image: a sweet smell lingers in the air while a warm body carries him up a flight of stairs, the sound of high heels echoing off cement walls. Someone falls over and Clarence begins to cry. When he reflected on it later in life, Clarence realized that this memory was probably of being with his grandmother in an apartment building near the Dare Foods factory in south Kitchener.

Another event, early on at the Reiers, showed that Clarence hadn't completely forgotten where he came from. One night someone broke into the Reiers' garden shed and stole some of their power tools. The Reiers called the police in the morning and an officer was sent to investigate. The moment Clarence spotted the police cruiser coming up the driveway, he ran and hid, completely overcome with fear.

> I don't know what kind of memory I had that was connected to that police car, but it was already ingrained in my mind.

To this day, when he unexpectedly encounters an officer of the law, Clarence sometimes still feels that jolt of terror.

As Clarence grew older, he started to think more often about his unusual situation. Something was not quite right. Despite the Reiers' care, despite the kinship of Margaret and Keith, Clarence knew deep down that he and his sister came from a different family, that they were outsiders. He was, after all, the Reiers' *foster* child. How does a young mind explain that situation to himself, explain why his *real* mother and father left him in the first place? Young Clarence could fathom only one explanation:

> It was really, really hard to come to terms with why I didn't have any parents. The terms that I came to, as to why I didn't have any parents, was that I must have been such a bad child that my parents didn't want me and they gave me up.

Clarence started looking for answers to his perceived problem. Something was missing, he knew that. The next step, then, was to go searching for the missing piece. One afternoon, he packed a little suitcase and snuck out of the house. From the kitchen window, Eileen watched her little boy drag his suitcase up the hill and sit down on it at the end of the drive. He sat there on his pack all afternoon, waiting for something which at the time he probably could not have described. When daylight waned, Ken went out to Clarence and brought him in for dinner, carrying his small suitcase back for him.

Abby Cachagee (1991)

The hardest thing was the loneliness of not knowing you had a home.

I can remember my grandfather paddling 900 miles every year to come up to the school fence and (this was around September — Yeah, the end of September he would show up). I could see him coming over up the embankment. He'd walk towards the fence, this huge tall man. He was well over six feet. And he had the smell of the bush, of fire, of animals to him. He would pass through the fence a little piece of dried meat. He wouldn't talk much. He would just look at us and try to touch us and feel us. Then he would disappear for another year. He did that for six years. He would come up every [year for] six years. Every Fall just to have -- we would line up against the fence, the four of us. He would talk to us in Indian. Sometimes my uncle would come. Then he would leave again for another year.

But the experience of that Indian school was basically loneliness, of wanting to get away, of wanting family, of wanting to go home, to have a place called home.[4]

MENNONITES

> It was a good upbringing on the farm, I never got hurt; I never got abused. But they were very strict, and it was a religious upbringing, because they were Mennonites.

Mennonites originated in Europe after the Protestant Reformation, emerging as a group of Christians that rebelled against the institutional church. They were persecuted for their unorthodox ways and soon gained a reputation for their pacifism, industrious farming skills, and insular communal living. Mennonite groups migrated to places all over the world where they were promised freedom of religion, exemption from military service, and economic opportunities. The first Mennonites who migrated to the Grand River Valley during the early nineteenth century were "Swiss" Mennonites from Pennsylvania. They had originally immigrated to North America from Switzerland and the Palatinate region of Germany.

In most cases, Mennonite settlers were invited or encouraged to migrate to newly created colonies of empires, in order to spread European agriculture techniques and Euro-Christian culture. Essentially, they were wanted to help colonize the land, which was usually accompanied by the displacement of its original inhabitants.

In both Pennsylvania and Ontario, Mennonite settlers had a complicated relationship with their Indigenous neighbours, to say the least. In the case of the settlement of the Grand River Valley, their colonization followed a common pattern. At first Mennonite settler relations with First Nations were generally cordial — they often engaged in mutual trade, for instance, and there is evidence of cultural exchange — but as the Mennonites became more permanently settled and more self-sufficient, a superiority complex emerged. As Christians, Mennonites were suspicious of Indigenous spirituality, which they understood as a "pagan" religion. Moreover, their agricultural methods were not compatible with traditional Indigenous land use. They began to deny Indigenous hunters access to the land or to clear-cut forests and plough fields to destroy traditional harvesting locations. Despite their non-violent aspirations, Mennonite settlers eventually helped the British colonial government in its ultimate mission to displace and dispossess the Haudenosaunee and Mississauga of their traditional territory in the Grand River Valley.

WHEN EUROPEAN SETTLERS began to colonize the Grand River Valley at the turn of the eighteenth century, Mississauga and Haudenosaunee First Nations were both living there, as they are to this day, abiding by the principles of the Dish with One Spoon Wampum. The Mississaugas used the upper part of the valley as traditional hunting grounds; and the Six Nations were living mostly on the lower portion, organized along the banks of the river in small villages according to the various nations of the Confederacy. The initial waves of settlers in the region were mainly comprised of Mennonite farmers from Pennsylvania.

After the American Revolution, land in Pennsylvania was at a premium. With their growing families, many Mennonites were drawn to Upper Canada by rumours of inexpensive property.[1]

Some of the first settlers to arrive colonized Block Number Two of the Haldimand Tract, a 60,000 acre portion of land, which had been acquired by a European land speculator on a lease arrangement with the Six Nations.[2] The original terms of this lease arrangement were intended for a duration of 999 years.

The early Mennonites settled in "parklike forest" on the "boundary area between forests and grassland."[3] They found rolling land with rich soil and plenty of tributaries, ideal for the kind of European agriculture that was their expertise. Whether they knew it or not (they likely would have) the existence of this ideal farming ground was in large part due to years of Indigenous land management — prescribed burns — conducted to form a habitat that encouraged the growth and proliferation of hunted species.[4]

Coming as they were with European notions of private property — land purchased to be used as the owner pleases — Mennonites settlers would not have been familiar with the principles of the One Dish, which governed the land upon which they settled as members of the British nation. They instead viewed this fertile and rich land as a divine gift to be enjoyed for their own prosperity, observing in it a resemblance to the ancient land of the Canaanites, flowing with milk and honey, promised to Abraham in their Holy Scriptures.[5]

Early Mennonite colonization attracted other immigrants (often of Germanic origin) and eventually, by means of fences or government enforcement, barred access to, or simply clear-cut, traditional hunting grounds of the Mississaugas and Haudenosaunee, displacing them and contributing to the dispossession of their traditional territory. Over the years, individual farms turned into settlements, and then towns, and most recently three cities — Kitchener, Waterloo, and Cambridge — subdivided many times over into many different lots, many separate dishes for many separate peoples.

THE REIERS BROUGHT Clarence and his sister to Mannheim Mennonite Church every Sunday, a yellow-brick building surrounded by cornfields just outside of the town of Mannheim. The church's rural congregation originated in the 1830s when Mennonite settlers in the area started to gather in their homes for worship.[6] Services began at 10:00 a.m. and would include hymn singing, Scripture readings, and a sermon.

At church Clarence learned to sing along to the hymns — he even briefly sang in the Inter-Mennonite Children's Choir when he was nine or ten. But the church setting, which required one to quietly remain seated for an extended period, was not particularly fitting for a boisterous child like Clarence; he often slipped off the old oak pews to run down the aisle and out of sight. Margaret recalls that he and his sister "were just all over the place." After church, the family would sometimes go for drives through the countryside in their Oldsmobile, traveling across the sprawling farmland of southern Ontario, the whole family packed into the car.

In their home, the Reiers prayed before meals and sometimes sang hymns together. During the summers, Clarence was sent to attend Bible School in the afternoons. Once he was old enough, he also recalls attending a Mennonite summer camp called Fraser Lake.

> You'd go for a week or ten days or something. I can remember Cheryl went before I did and then she came back and she had all these stories, and, oh, it was so much fun. And then a year or two later, I was able to go.

Reflecting on the summer camps, Clarence recalls,

> I don't think I really felt out of place, and I didn't have any separation anxiety like some kids did. It was

just another place where I was put. But as I got older, it was fun. Camp was fun.

In regards to the Christian teachings at summer camps and Bible school, Clarence explains,

> I kind of phased all that stuff out. Bible School was Bible School. Did I retain anything? No.

Just because they were Mennonites did not mean that the Reiers traveled in horse and buggy or followed a strict dress code. In fact, they dressed much like their non-Mennonite neighbours and were happy to get around with the help of internal combustion engines. This is because the Reiers were not Old Order Mennonites.

In 1889 there was a schism in the Mennonite community in Ontario, a split between traditional and more liberal groupings.[7] The traditionalists were generally opposed to technological and societal change, preferring not to adopt certain new technology and deciding to continue to use their German language for church services, rather than English. Now known as Old Order Mennonites, they continue to speak a distinct German dialect, wear nineteenth-century garments, and use horse-power for travel and farming.

But the "new order" Mennonites were less opposed to adopting the trends and technologies of the changing world around them. Although, especially in the early twentieth century, it would still be fair to consider them a relatively conservative community. For instance, at that time — as in the Old Order community — Mennonite children rarely continued past grade eight in the public education system. When Eileen was a young girl, her teacher had called home trying to persuade her parents to let her continue into high school — she was an excellent student. Eileen overheard the conversation and never forgot what her father had said: "No, she's needed on the farm."[8]

When it came to going to church or sending him to Christian camp, there was no question about it — the Reiers were Christians, and it seemed appropriate to raise their foster children in the Christian faith. Although Clarence did not retain much of the Christian beliefs of his foster family, he was certainly influenced by their culture. He traces his work ethic to his experience on the farm, following the lead of his foster father and older brother. Ken Reier taught Clarence, from an early age, to be seen and not heard and to speak when spoken to — in other words, to respect your elders and to hold the community above the individual; values that Clarence identifies with today.

It wasn't until Clarence was ten years old that he began asking his social workers questions about his identity, only to get short and cryptic responses regarding his absent parents and "Native blood." When Clarence had become a Crown Ward in 1967, the social workers and supervisors in charge of him were not concerned with preserving his Indigenous identity or culture. Records show that they knew that Clarence and his sister had membership to Chapleau Cree First Nation, however they assumed that assimilation into the dominant Euro-Canadian culture would necessarily make a better life for the children, as one CAS worker wrote in Clarence's file: "We often provide foster homes for Indian children, and this procedure is certainly the best one for young children." And the non-Indigenous parents who adopted Indigenous children or provided foster care, for the most part, shared these beliefs. Mennonites were no exception.

THE FEDERAL GOVERNMENT began winding down its Indian Residential Schools in the early 1950s, recognizing their overall failure and intending to transfer Indigenous children to the provincial public education systems. In 1951, the Indian Act was amended to allow provinces to provide child welfare services for Indigenous children, and within the decade, the rate of Indigenous children in child welfare exponentially increased. The practice in

Canada of taking Indigenous children from their families, especially on reserves, and putting them into adoptive or foster care with, in most cases, non-Indigenous families — and sometimes families outside of Canada in Europe or America — has come to be known as the Sixties Scoop.

Generally referring to the time period of the 1960s-90s, the term first appeared in Patrick Johnston's 1983 report *Native Children and the Child Welfare System*, which outlined the highly disproportionate number of Indigenous children registered in Canada's child welfare systems, a pattern that continues to this day. Johnston argued that the cause of this over-representation is complex, identifying a few key factors: disagreements between the provincial and federal governments on responsibility and funding for Indigenous children; cultural insensitivity of social workers who lacked understanding of Indigenous cultures; poverty; and the legacy of colonialism and especially the residential schools, which often resulted in alcohol use and gave officials an excuse to take children from their families.[9]

Johnston noted that for some Indigenous families, the government's failure to provide child welfare amounted to infanticide.[10] Other scholars at the time and presently argued that cultural genocide was at work: the welfare system was continuing the racist and colonial effort of residential schools attempting to erase Indigenous identity through relocation and assimilation.[11] Canada's Truth and Reconciliation Commission came to a similar conclusion in 2015, noting that the Sixties Scoop "was in some measure simply a transferring of children from one form of institution, the residential school, to another, the child welfare agency."[12] The welfare system closely followed the logic of the schools in their presumption that Indigenous children needed saving from a purportedly inferior culture and should be assimilated into mainstream society. Social workers mimicked the dangerous precedent of schools when they forcibly removed children from their homes and reserves to isolate them from cultural influence in non-Indigenous homes.[13] The almost non-existent concern for preservation of cultural identity speaks to the predominance of racist attitudes among Canadian society during this time. Although not all Indigenous children had fully negative experiences in adoption or foster care — and certainly some were in need of intervention when child welfare became involved — most Indigenous children who were involved in child welfare experienced a similar impact on their lives as the children who survived the residential schools: they became alienated from their identity and struggled to cope with life.[14]

Despite decades of research and advocacy, the Canadian governments did not address its failure to provide culturally sensitive child welfare for Indigenous children. In 2017, after an eight year court trial, the government finally announced an $800 million settlement of a class action lawsuit launched on behalf of Sixties Scoop Survivors; the money was a form of compensation for the survivors' loss of cultural identity.[15]

Clarence's experience illustrates the complexity of being involved in the Sixties Scoop. For one, he experienced the trauma all children experience when they are displaced from their parents, and also importantly, the impact on Clarence was compounded when culture and extended family were removed. His situation also shows how there are different degrees of consent involved with the parents of children involved in the Sixties Scoop. Clarence was not, after all, taken forcibly from his reserve, as was often the case with other Indigenous children. His mother Maureen — reluctantly and with great sorrow — did agree to give him up along with his sister; although it is clear that a failure of social and community services put her in a situation where she did not have much of a choice. She was in a state of poverty and suffered from multiple health issues, falling through the cracks of social support and finding herself unable to provide shelter and safety for her children. And when it comes to Clarence's father, Abby, there is no doubt that the legacy of residential schools had a major impact on him as a young father; he was suffering greatly from his childhood experiences. His mental health challenges, alcohol use and involvement with crime, ultimately meant he was unable to be a fully present and supportive parent, despite indicating this desire on multiple occasions. All these factors led Clarence into the care of CAS and, like his father and grandmother before him, he found himself in a system that cut him off from his Cree culture and family.

It was admirable for the Reiers to open their home to two displaced children. And Clarence attests to their loving care and support — as Margaret put it, for Ken and Eileen "their kids came first, and that included Cheryl and Mike." But the Reiers also came from a cultural context, the Mennonite community and Canada at large, that mistakenly assumed Euro-Christian culture was superior to Indigenous culture. Indeed, up to the 1980s, many Ontario Mennonites actively supported Mennonite-led residential schools in northern Ontario.[16] Like so many other adoptive or fostering families of Indigenous children, the Reiers were not prepared to teach Clarence about his history or help him learn about his culture. It was simply never acknowledged. And in this way, the Reiers, with all of their good and honest intentions, participated in a government-supported system that erased Indigenous identity by means of assimilation.

> We're not saying this to tarnish the name of the Reiers. The Reiers did the best they could with what they had, and for that I'm grateful. But this is a real life event. People unwittingly participate in unjust systems. The only way to change these systems is to stop supporting them.

As a young child, Clarence always remembered the time before living with the Reiers. And those unattended memories of abandonment eventually turned into a core piece of his identity.

> When I reflect back, I had a good upbringing, compared to some children. It's just all those internalized feelings that had an effect on me.

IT HAPPENED ONE AUTUMN DAY, likely in 1973 when Clarence was eight. The mild weather had yet to give way to the bite of winter, and Clarence and Cheryl took their time meandering home from the school bus stop.

> I can remember we'd always play in the ditches. We'd always play hide-and-go-seek, or we'd just skip stones, or just be kids.

But this time as they were playing, they stumbled upon something abandoned in the ditch.

> We found half a case of Labatt's Blue, little stubby pilsner bottles. We figured out how to get the caps off using a nearby fence. Had one beer and then another. After about one or two beers I felt different. I felt okay. I didn't feel scared. I didn't feel worried. I didn't feel out of place. I had a sense of calmness over me. I knew from that day on that whatever liquid was in that little brown bottle would help me cope and help me feel okay.

Clarence and Keith Reier, Ken Reier behind

Abby Cachagee (1991)

We used to make shacks out in the bush here. In the back, way in the back there. We would haul stuff back from the dump, stoves and chairs and couches and car seats and tables. We'd set up our shacks and they would be little houses all through the bush. And many times we'd have our snares back there too. So we had red meat on a few occasions.

From the chicken house, we would stew the chickens out there and take them out to the back of the bush and cook 'em up and boil 'em up. We would sometimes stew — they were just making the Hydro lines way out in the back there, and the construction crews would hide beer out in the bush and we would look at where they had hid, take the beer and come back here and drink it.

That's where I think that many of us started our earlier drinking experiences, was at the Indian school. Because I noticed a lot of the older boys then started buying wine, started drinking wine. Or we would get a person downtown, one of the local street people there, to buy us some wine and bring it back. And if we couldn't find anybody to buy us wine, we'd go into the drugstore and what was called beef-ironing wine. And if you drank the whole bottle and kept it down, it was okay, but half the time you'd throw it up again, so you'd have to keep doing it. So there quite a few of us who started out as early drinkers.

4

THE WESTERN DOOR

> The Bear Skull is a sacred item because I feel that it is connected to my spirit. The skull has medicinal properties. It keeps me connected to the clan that I'm from. The bear is a protector of its cubs. It keeps me connected to the Western Doorway where my ancestors are.

Since time immemorial, the Cree people[1] have lived on and taken care of a vast territory of land along the south-west coast of James Bay and Hudson Bay. The land has and continues to provide everything needed for living.[2]

Clarence's ancestry traces back to a Cree family group that lived inland. Historically, his ancestors practiced a semi-nomadic way of life. Most of the year was spent on the land hundreds of kilometres upstream from the bay, where marshy swampland transitions into boreal forest. They used to annually travel up and down the rivers that feed into the great bays, spending winters inland in the forest and then, when summer approached, heading downstream (northward) for gatherings on the bay's shore.

Each year followed this cycle of activity that saw them travelling several hundreds of kilometres on foot and by canoe. The winter was spent hunting and trapping, living off the land and food stores from the previous year, and trading with (typically) Anishinaabe who were located at the southern limits of their territory. When spring came — known as the season when deer walk — caribou migrate southwards back to their traditional feeding grounds. To capture them, Cree hunters traditionally raised long deer hedges, fences extending for several kilometres that siphoned the deer into traps. Caribou meat was preserved by being cut into thin slices that are then cured in the sun or over a fire. This dried meat was sometimes pounded between stones into a fine powder called Ruhiggan and could keep for years without spoiling.[3] Ruhiggan mixed with fat and berries is a Cree delicacy.

The spring ice break-up heralds the fish spawning runs. Suckers, lake sturgeons, and pike can be trapped with fish weirs and fishing nets, or sometimes, in the case of large sturgeon, they could even be speared. As the weather warms, the geese leave the coast and head inland to nest. Geese arrive around the time of the Goose Moon (April) and are another important source of sustenance. According to the Cree worldview, every animal possesses personhood. Therefore, it is the animal who determines the success of the hunt, not the hunter. One honours captured animals by using all parts of their bodies and by only harvesting as much as is needed for survival. Spring thaw also loosens the sap of the Maple and Birch trees, which can be collected and rendered, either through freezing or boiling, into sweet syrup. If one knew where to look and how to see, they would find plenty of edible plants in the region. Berries, which can be dried and stored to be kept for the months ahead, are especially prolific. Many different types of plants also have medicinal and ceremonial uses.

Once the rivers thawed, the inland Cree began their long canoe trip downstream (northward) to the James Bay shores. After a winter living on the land, Cree families happily reunited with relatives and friends to socialize, trade, and celebrate. Festivities consisted of feasts, games, singing, storytelling, and traditional ceremonies. This was also a chance to renew relationships, work through disputes, and discuss foreign relations. Like other family groups, Clarence's ancestors had a hunting territory, associated with a river system, the limits of which were negotiated during these summer gatherings. The James Bay shores are therefore an important and historical gathering place for the Cree.[4]

After a summer spent by the bay, they left again for their winter hunting grounds, bringing food stores, such as root vegetables and dried meat, as well as goods to trade with neighbouring nations to the south or fellow Cree to the north. In this way, they acted as intermediaries in an ancient trade economy. Before European contact, trade networks connecting to James Bay reached as far as Lake Superior, the St Lawrence, and even Mexico.

By the early 1600s, acting as agents, the Cree were trading European-manufactured goods that originally came from French traders who had sailed up what is known as the St Lawrence River. However, in 1669, the Cree encountered Europeans for the first time: British traders, employed by the Hudson's Bay Company, had managed to navigate into Hudson Bay and sail down to the shores of James Bay.

HBC traders sought mainly beaver, fox, and mink pelts, which were highly valuable commodities in Europe; Cree traders likewise valued European-manufactured goods, such as metal tools, textiles, and guns. Relationships developed along with trade and, not surprisingly, contact between such distinct cultures soon began to change both peoples — materially, culturally, and spiritually.

Over the next several years, the Hudson's Bay Company (HBC) established a series of trading posts along the shores of the bays. The fur trade proved to be a lucrative business, so much so that British and French forces skirmished regularly for access to the region. By 1716, their relations had normalized and the HBC began building more permanent trading posts, called factories, near the mouths of geographically important rivers feeding into the

James and Hudson Bays. Moose Factory appeared during this time on Moose Island, near the mouth of Moose River.

Some Cree participated in the trade economy more than others; they spent increasingly more time close to the factories and intermarried with HBC traders. Others, including Clarence's ancestors, continued to practice their usual way of life, acting as agents in the modified trade economy, trading with Anishinaabe to the south and transporting goods to the coast for profit. As for European traders who lived at the various HBC factories on the bay, they quickly learned that they had to adapt to Indigenous ways of living and being in order to survive on the land.

As HBC traders became more familiar with local Cree hunters, they began to advance goods to them, using debt to ensure a steady supply of fur. At the end of the winter, certain hunters were furnished with supplies, with the expectation that these would be paid for with next year's harvest.

This intercontinental trade economy carried on for many years. However, after nearly a century of trading on the coast, the HBC began to push its trading posts inland. This was done largely in response to competition from private traders, mainly French Canadians, who had made their way into the interior via the Great Lakes and their river systems. In 1779, these private traders incorporated as the North West Company. Competitive prices at inland posts drew some Cree families to the south, or, in the case of those located mainly inland, who traversed annually the river systems feeding the Bays, the existence of southern trade options motivated them to spend more time at their winter hunting grounds.

By 1777, there was an HBC trading post on Missinaibi Lake, near the height of the Arctic Watershed. Another post had also been established near a town that would soon come to be known as Chapleau. It is around this time that we can pick up the story of one family line in Clarence's ancestry — the Saylors.

CLARENCE'S PATERNAL GREAT, great grandparents, Jacob Saylors and his wife Rachel (née Goodwin), were Inland Cree, part of a family that, in the early nineteenth century, was living traditionally on the land and trading at the HBC post near Chapleau. The Saylors' traditional hunting territory is located within the Moose River Basin. The Saylors would have belonged to a close-knit family group who likely identified with the river system where the family hunted and resided — in his case, the Missinaibi River, which runs nearly 800 kilometres from Missinaibi Lake (northwest of Chapleau) to join with Moose River shortly before feeding into James Bay. Family group hunting territories had flexible boundaries, usually defined loosely around a drainage system into a main river.[5] The Moose River Basin is mostly flat wetland consisting of swamp or muskeg. Hundreds of kilometres upstream (southward) from James Bay, this lowland increases in elevation and transitions into boreal forest. Jacob's family practiced that semi-nomadic way of life that involved wintering inland and then travelling to the James Bay coast, likely near Moose Factory Post, for annual trading, celebrations, and ceremonies.

The Saylors would have been physically, emotionally, spiritually, and mentally connected to the land. Navigating their canoes down the Missinaibi River until it joins with the Moose River, the Saylors would have carried with them an assortment of goods for trade: pelts of many types, maple syrup, and other crafted items, for example. The family navigated two worlds: the world of traditional subsistence land-use, and the world of cross-continental trade.

A small colony of settlers had established the town of Chapleau near the southern limit of the Saylors' traditional territory. Just on the outskirts of the town was a small HBC trading post. The Saylors were clearly familiar with settlers at the post because Jacob and Rachel's son, Isaiah, formed a relationship with Mary McLeod, the daughter of an HBC trader. They married and raised ten children. During Isaiah's lifetime, the Saylors, along with other Cree family groups, began to spend more time inland at the south end of the Missinaibi river system. They were drawn there by changing economic and geographic conditions. Competition for furs was depleting game reserves; at the same time, demand for furs in Europe was diminishing. Some Cree families could no longer sustain themselves through subsistence hunting and trading; they began working in settler towns. Isaiah Saylors, for example, was employed as a tally-man at the Chapleau trading post. He was also a local Cree leader.

By the turn of the nineteenth century, European colonization was causing drastic changes in the area. The newly-laid Canadian Pacific Railway (CPR) brought more European settlers to town: prospectors, foresters, and hunters, all looking to make a profit from what they saw as limitless natural resources there for the taking. The CPR also constructed a steam engine refuelling point and repair shops in Chapleau. In turn, the town's settler population grew quickly.

Throughout these changes, the Chapleau Cree continued to make the annual journey to James Bay, to trade and to stay connected with family and friends up north.[6] Among the Chapleau Cree is included Clarence's ancestors: the Saylors and Cachagees. His lineage is as follows: Isaiah Saylors and Mary McLeod were the parents of Charles Saylors; Charles Saylors and Helen Chappise were the parents of Margaret Saylors; Margaret Saylors and Howard Cachagee were the parents of Clarence's father: Clarence "Abby" Cachagee.

In 1870, keen to gain control of the land for European settlement and resource development, the Canadian government began making treaties with First Nations who lived in territories that government leaders deemed important to the growth of the new state. Called the Numbered Treaties, these eleven treaties were signed between 1871 and 1922. A treaty was the foundation of respectful partnerships between First Nations and Europeans that would ensure mutual benefits. The terms of the Numbered Treaties generally promised Indigenous signatories a series of benefits: initial cash payments, ongoing annuities, hunting and fishing rights, and reserved lands in return for government title to the land. In reality, the Canadian government used the Numbered Treaties to defraud First Nations of their title to the land so the nation-state could profit from resource extraction. The treaties also paved the way for European society to assimilate Indigenous Peoples into mainstream society.

With the fur trade declining and white settlement growing near the end of the nineteenth century, Cree and Anishinaabe First Nations located in northern Ontario requested that the Canadian government make a treaty with them. In short, like their neighbours to the south who had already signed treaties, they wanted financial compensation for sharing the land as well as protection from future resource development.[7] First Nation families that were situated on the south end of the arctic watershed, such as the Saylors and Cachagees, were especially concerned about resource development because they were witnessing the front lines of settler encroachment into their territory.

In 1901, the federal and provincial governments began drafting Treaty Number Nine, meant to cover unceded territory in northern Ontario. Within a couple years the document was completed, all before any of the commissioners had even met with First Nations leaders. The words of the treaty outlined in typical legalese a wholesale release of Indigenous rights to the land. In return, the document promised continued harvesting rights (subject to qualifications), reserve lands (to be determined by the commissioners),[8] initial cash payments, ongoing annuities, and funds for the provision of education.[9] The Ontario government added a clause that prohibited the establishment of reserves on rivers that had good potential for hydroelectric power generation, a colonial policy that purposely excluded First Nations from sharing in the wealth of resource development. There was no intention on the government's part to negotiate any of these terms.

In 1905, Duncan Campbell Scott and two other commissioners, one federal and one provincial, set out on a tour of northern Ontario to make a treaty with the various Anishinaabe and Cree communities in the area. None of the commissioners spoke the Anishinaabe or Cree languages so they had to rely on translators to explain the terms of the treaty. It is also clear from their own journals that they had no intention of explaining the treaty in detail.[10] As a result, what was verbally explained and promised to Anishinaabe and Cree leaders was significantly different from what was written in the document.[11]

The commissioners described the treaty as one of peace and friendship. Cash payments and annuities were characterized as expressions of good will. Upon meeting with the commissioners, one of the primary concerns expressed by Indigenous leaders was that their people would continue to be free to live off of the land. In response, the commissioners reassured them that reserves would be set aside as a place where no settler would be allowed to disturb them and that they would be guaranteed free movement.

It wasn't until 1906, on a second tour of northern Ontario, that the commissioners came into contact with Clarence's ancestors and other family groups that would eventually make up Chapleau Cree First Nation. Among those Cree leaders who met with the commissioners near the town of Chapleau was Isaiah Saylors. Because Inland Cree spoke the same dialect of Cree that is spoken in Moose Factory area, the commissioner assumed that they were a part of that nation. Duncan wrote in his final report: "It was not necessary to make treaty with the Indians of Chapleau, as they belong to bands residing at Moose Factory, English River, and other points where a treaty had already been made. They were, however, recognized as members of the bands to which they belong, and were paid the gratuity due them, after being informed as to what the acceptance of the money by them involved."[12]

We must take stock of the fact that when Scott claims that the Chapleau Cree were *informed* of what acceptance of payments meant, he glosses over the fact that he spoke through a translator in terms undoubtedly similar to those used in the previous year — that is, Isaiah Saylors and others were told that they would be free to continue hunting and harvesting from the land, while a reserve would be established for their exclusive use.

The commissioner decided that the land they met upon — likely at the old Chapleau trading post just east of the town — would be staked out as a reserve for the Chapleau Cree. Consultation with First Nations was not a government priority during treaty making; the commissioners' goal was to gain signatures, not input. After being surveyed the reserve amounted to one hundred and sixty acres, and sat on a peninsula between the Kebsquasheshing (Chapleau) and Nebskwashi Rivers.

The Saylors were one of the first families to live on the reserve. However, it soon became apparent that the land was of poor quality. Because it was situated on a peninsula between two rivers, it was prone to flooding in the spring; the reserve was also downstream from Chapleau where the CPR had built a refuelling and repair station, which, along with sewage from the town, polluted the river. It was not long before the Chapleau Cree began to suffer the effects of contaminated water. Seeking new employment and better living conditions, community members increasingly migrated into the town of Chapleau.

Although some Chapleau Cree continued to live off the land and trade furs, competition from settlers and years of over-harvesting were causing an alarming depletion of game reserves. At the same time, only a few years after the signing of Treaty Nine, the Ontario government began to deny the Chapleau Cree their right to hunt and fish on their land. The government's disregard for Indigenous treaty rights is perhaps best illustrated by the Chapleau Game Preserve, created in 1925.

The Preserve was originally the idea of William McLeod (not related to Mary McLeod, the wife of Isaiah Saylors). William ran a fur trading store in Chapleau during the early 1900s. As a fur trader himself, he was familiar with the depleting game reserves in the area and the impact this was having on local harvesters. He proposed that the Ontario government establish a game preserve to provide a sanctuary for animal life.[13] Eventually, William's idea took root and turned into one of the largest game preserves in North America. But contrary to William's initial intention that the preserve should respect Indigenous rights to hunt and survive off the land, when the government chose the location for the preserve, they ignored its potential impact on First Nations within and at the edge of the preserve's boundary: one Anishinaabe reserve was even surrounded by the preserve. Realizing their error after the fact, the government forcibly relocated the First Nation to the shores of an isolated lake nearly 60 kilometres away. In the case of the Chapleau Cree, who were situated at the southern edge of the preserve, a large portion of their traditional hunting grounds was suddenly made off-limits. The government broke its promises only nineteen years after making them.

From the early 1900s to the 1950s, a series of factors worked to disintegrate the Chapleau Cree community. Colonial government oppression by means of oppressive policies, such as the residential school system and denial of treaty rights, worked to disperse Chapleau Cree families and halt the intergenerational transmission of culture and identity. Depleting game reserves made traditional subsistence living increasingly difficult, while water pollution from the town made living on the reserve less tolerable. Additionally, two world wars caused family stress and dysfunction. The last Chapleau Cree trapper passed away before the middle of the twentieth century, leaving the reserve essentially abandoned. Nearly thirty years passed before the Chapleau Cree First Nation reorganized at Fox Lake.

5

DISCONNECTING

Clarence remembers the years 1976 and 1977 with fond feelings. He was eleven and had a growth spurt, suddenly finding that he excelled in athletics. He once challenged his Phys-Ed. teacher to a race across the field and almost won. In the school's track-and-field competition, he competed in the hundred- and two-hundred metre dashes and the pentathlon. A few years later, in grade eight, he won first place in the pentathlon for the Waterloo region.

But at the same time, entering those teenage years life became, as Clarence puts it, a little "hectic." He was hanging out with a crew of young boys who had a knack for trouble-making — usually aided and abetted by substance use. He started experimenting with cannabis at this time. The first time he smoked was with a friend at the New Dundee dam; when it took effect he felt queasy and vomited — it wasn't exactly what he had expected.

In those days, if Clarence wanted to meet up with his friends from town, he cut through the forests and fields between the farm and the town; the roads were much less direct. It wasn't so bad heading into town when there was still daylight, but it was usually dark by the time he came home — no doubt to the alarm of the Reiers. Clarence remembers one night in the summer of '77. He and his friends probably had been playing one of their favourite pranks: they would all pretend to beat up on one of their crew in full view of a passerby, intending to have the concerned citizen call the police and send them on a wild chase. The one left behind had to make up some convincing story about suddenly being attacked by a gang of youth.

It was unusually windy on the walk home that night. As Clarence left the dirt roads to cut through fields and bushes, he thought about how he had always felt comfortable in nature. Sometimes he wondered if this was somehow connected to his Indigenous roots.

The previous year, he had asked his social workers about his biological family.

> All that they disclosed to us was brief information about them; all they said about our mom was that her last name was Lindsay. No information other than that. Any information they gave us about our father was that he was a Native and that he was an alcoholic, either dead or living on the streets of Toronto.

They did not tell him that his father's last name, Cachagee, meant crow, which was his family emblem and spirit animal. They did not say that he belonged to the Chapleau Cree First Nation. No one was there to share the stories of his people, no one to teach him how to live off the land, how to play the drum and sing traditional songs. No, they did not share these things with him. All they said was that his father was a deadbeat.

> When you hear stuff like that, it's pretty much hearing that your parent is the lowest of the low. And then where do you fit in when you hear stuff like that?

Rows of corn stalks bowed to gusts of wind. Moonlit depressions ribboned across fields of grass. In the bush between parcels of farmland, the trees shook off their dead limbs.

Clarence recalls walking home to the Reiers that terribly windy night. On his way home he paused amidst the windstorm and shouted into the darkness, challenging all that it stood for. His cry joined the chorus of whistling leaves and creaking trunks.

 I took my abandonment issues — of not having any parents — and I buried those deep down inside of me, because that affected me in a horrible, horrible way.

"YES, it's the Mike you know," Eileen used to admit into the telephone receiver with some hesitation, embarrassed that her foster son, only recently a teenager, already had a reputation with the Waterloo Region Police Force. The Reiers were required by law to inform the police whenever their foster children went missing. It was usually only a matter of time before a social worker or police officer would find Clarence roaming the streets with a group of friends, or he would be identified after getting into trouble. After each incident, as punishment, CAS would place Clarence in a group home temporarily before returning him to the Reiers' care. By the time he was fifteen years old, Clarence had been placed in five different group homes, usually a different one each time he ran away from the farm.

 Reflecting back, I don't really think I was running away. I was running *to*. I think I was running to find what I was connected to, what I belonged to, because I knew that where I was staying, that they were my foster parents, yes, but that wasn't really my family and that's not really where I belonged.

The first time Clarence actually ran away from home was one

night in 1976 when he was eleven years old. He climbed down the
T.V. antenna beside the farmhouse, positioned conveniently close
to the window of his second-floor room. He doesn't remember
exactly where he went, possibly he walked to the main road
through New Dundee and met up with some friends.

Running away — or running to — soon turned into a repeat
occurrence. In November 1978, CAS records report an incident in
which Clarence and one of his friends took the Reiers' vehicle and
"went absent without leave for a few days."[1] Clarence remembers
that differently. When the Reiers went out for a night, Clarence
and a friend took the Reiers' Olds *Toronado* out for a ride. As he
recalls it, they went to the next town over and came back that
night. His parents weren't pleased, and the next day he had to give
the car a good wash.

As he grew into adolescence, Clarence began to misbehave
more often. He started stealing from others. He remembers
scrounging through his foster grandma's purse and wallet while she
was distracted visiting with the Reiers. Asked what compelled him
to act in this way, Clarence responds:

> I don't know why; I just had this thing where I didn't
> care about people. I didn't care about what they
> owned. I didn't care about how hard they worked for
> things. If I wanted something back then, I would
> break in and I would get it. I would do break and
> enters. I would steal from people.

He even once helped himself from the offering plate at church,
a decision which he admits did cause him some consternation:

> I thought about that for many years. You know, if
> there is a god, am I going to pay for that, with karma?

Tensions between Clarence and his parents grew strained
until, in February 1979, Clarence's parents requested that CAS

place him in an emergency group home, which happened to be in the nearby town of St Agatha. At the same time, in an effort to regain a trusting relationship, the Reiers and Clarence also started counseling sessions together. But it was not especially helpful. As Clarence recalls, his experience at school struggling to learn and being an outcast, combined with his deteriorating relationship with the Reiers, became overwhelming.

> These things just started to layer and layer and layer on top of each other. And then before you knew it, I became kind of calloused. And what I did to protect myself when I was in trouble: I just disconnected. I wouldn't say anything, and I just put myself in a little box.

By the summer of that year, Clarence was back home on the farm, helping with chores once again.

> I'm now grateful that they took us in, but at that time, the identity hole was starting to bleed because there were so many unanswered questions. Why was I here? Why was I a Crown Ward? Why didn't I know who my parents were?

Those unanswered questions could begin to explain some of the decisions that Clarence made at the time. He recalls one famous story (among the Reiers, that is) of the shenanigans that he got up to.

One of the Reiers' adult daughters lived in a smaller house on the property; she had moved into this home recently after being married. Clarence happened to be aware that there was a stash of homebrewed wine in his foster sister's basement. So one day, when she was preoccupied at the hospital giving birth to her first child, Clarence and two of his friends snuck into her house and made off with some alcoholic spoils. Six bottles of wine in tow, the teenage boys hiked to a favourite fishing spot. They drank into the evening, and by the time it was dark and they were ready to go home, the teenage trio was, as Clarence puts it, "all loaded and stupefied." After falling into the creek and tripping over an electric fence, they finally made it back to the barn, where they were soon discovered.

> We were all swaying back and forth and we weren't making much sense... I can remember Ken and Eileen just kind of smirking and shaking their heads. We were dripping wet and very inebriated.

The Reiers telephoned Clarence's friends' parents who came and brought them home and then Clarence was sent to bed. Unfortunately, the story doesn't end there. He woke up that night feeling nauseous, stuck his head out the window, and proceeded to stain purple an exterior wall of the white-siding farmhouse.

At the end of that summer, Clarence got into more serious trouble. After running away one day, he met up with some city friends and they broke into a couple different homes in Kitchener. Clarence was caught soon after. The Reiers had recently informed CAS that they were concerned about Clarence stealing money and alcohol from the house and from friends. He was consequently sentenced to stay at a youth detention centre located on the corner of Church and Benton Streets in downtown Kitchener.

> I remember being taken there by the police and then doing my intake. I was quiet. It was a foreign place, but I remember there were other youth there, boys and girls segregated. It was a big house.

On April 7, 1980, after a couple months living in the detention centre, Clarence was returned to the care of the Reiers. Five days later he was gone again, this time together with his sister. After the two were located, CAS put Clarence back into the group home in St Agatha. Clarence has a clear memory of one thing in particular at this group home: there were goats in the back of the property and the children staying at the home helped take care of them. While he was there, he learned one advantage to being assigned that chore. After secretly sharing cigarettes behind the shed, some of the boys fed the butts to the goats. "Goats eat anything," explained the oldest. "They get rid of the evidence."

Clarence made a lot of new friends during his stays at group homes. Once back home at the Reiers he would continue to meet up with his new friends in the city. At first, being in and out of these new living situations caused Clarence some distress, but soon he grew used to a life in flux.

> It wasn't fun in those homes, but it was okay. I never got beaten. I never got abused. They fed us. I always felt like a victim of change. So when I would get taken to these group homes, I'd be scared, I'd be shy. I didn't like going to them. But it seemed like after a while, it became the norm, just because I got moved around so much. And whenever I ran away, that's where I'd end up.

By the summer of 1980, when Clarence was fourteen, his relationship with his foster parents was especially strained. The Reiers were concerned about his drug use, so they had arranged for more counselling sessions for Clarence individually as well as sessions with the Reiers. In a report to CAS, the counsellor who saw Clarence noted: "Mike has had no difficulty in expressing his feelings to me. He, however, has not been able to share his feelings with you [the CAS social worker] and Mr. and Mrs. Reier." Later the counsellor wrote, "He is somewhat concerned about his own identity and is thinking about the possibility of making contact, someday, with his natural parents." Clarence reflects on his relationship with the Reiers at the time:

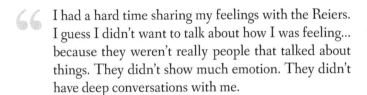

> I had a hard time sharing my feelings with the Reiers.
> I guess I didn't want to talk about how I was feeling...
> because they weren't really people that talked about
> things. They didn't show much emotion. They didn't
> have deep conversations with me.

In the midst of this, Clarence was in Junior high school, grade 7 at Queensmount, and during grade 8 he attended Wilmot Senior School. He recalls still struggling with classwork at this age — not being able to pay attention and having difficulty comprehending the lessons. But it was at Wilmot Senior, in grade eight, that Clarence would happen to become friends with someone who would go on to play an important role in his life. There was a Catholic school in St Agatha that had an arrangement with Wilmot Senior in which their grade 7 and 8 students would visit the school certain days of the week for home economics and shop class. One student from the Catholic school was Stephanie. As Clarence recalls:

> I used to hang out with Steph's brother and that's
> how I met her the first time. Then I would see her on
> and off when they would come to our school for
> Home-Ec.

They both soon took an interest in each other. At that time, the Reiers' farm was hooked into a communal telephone line. Clarence remembers receiving prank phone calls: "They'd call, and they'd hang up or they'd ask for me. Steph would call with her friends and talk to me and try to make me figure out who it was. Yeah, it was kind of fun." To tell the truth, Clarence and Stephanie were at first only friends — her romantic interest was for one of Clarence's friends — but the situation changed when they went to high school together.

In 1980, sporting an afro — a sure sign of the times — Clarence entered high school at Waterloo Oxford. He enrolled into the occupational stream and, surprising himself as well as his teachers, he excelled in his classes. Within a month, he was fast-tracked to grade ten. At the same time Clarence made some new friends and started experimenting with hallucinogenic drugs.

> I can remember in grade seven or eight they'd always say that cannabis is a gateway drug. Well it was. First I was drinking. Then I was smoking a bit of reefer. Then it was doing LSD, dropping acid.

One popular weekend activity that Clarence recalls involved picking up a case of beer with his friends and then driving out to Bingeman's for roller skating. These were the kinds of social events where Clarence got to spend more time with Stephanie. They started dating after going on a few double-dates with mutual friends, which included seeing in theatres the hit movie *9 to 5*, starring Dolly Parton.

> I think we always knew that we liked each other. We always had that connection, that chemistry.
>
> When I was young, I made a lot of wrong choices. I can remember in grade ten I went out for a cigarette, out into the smoking compound, one day. And I never came back again. I think I even remember telling Steph I was going out for a cigarette. And I never came back again. We were supposedly dating but, yeah, that's when I think I ran away. Ran away from school. Ran away from home.

As was becoming the pattern, after running away and staying with friends, Clarence would eventually come back to the farm. He recalls:

> The farm was a stable place because it was the only place that I knew that was consistent in my life. There was a level of comfort there, but it seemed only for a limited amount of time, until I wanted to run away again.

Keith had an old Datsun B-210, a small two-door car that was, as Clarence describes it, "pukey yellow." It was not in the best shape; snow blew in through the vents on the way to church. But after purchasing a new car, Keith parked the Datsun between the two barns on the farm property. It sat there for a couple years, collecting dust. One day Clarence asked if he could have the car and Keith agreed; he wasn't using it after all. "It blew my mind," says Clarence. "I was just overjoyed."

> I hung out with buddies back then who all had their own cars. That car, the first thing we did with it was crawl under it and rip the exhaust off of it, to make it sound loud, make it sound cool and powerful; meanwhile it was just a shitbox four-cylinder.

Clarence called up a friend and they took it out for a ride in the back flats. They drove it so hard that the front shocks came right through the hood. Ken rewelded the suspension at least once. Cheryl even took it out for a spin with her friends a couple times. Clarence recalls that neighbours called at least once to ask if the Reiers knew that someone was joyriding in their back fields. Needless to say, it didn't take long for Clarence to put the car out of commission — but he had a lot of fun doing it.

Later that summer Cheryl ran away, which caused Clarence to feel especially isolated at the farm. At the same time, Clarence's late nights out and random days missing was a source of frustration for the Reiers. He remembers that they used to lean a board up against the front door from the inside, so that when he came home late at night, it would fall over and alert them that he had returned.

One night he came home and tried to sneak in (the Reiers never locked the house), explaining:

> When you're a kid you know the house so well that you can maneuver it so well (which steps creak and all that). I was not expecting the table leaf to be propped up against the door. It slid down and went BOOM. Scared the crap out of me.

A light turned on in the room and Ken appeared.

> It was normally mom who would have those conversations with me, so for Ken to come out right away, it was: 'uh-oh, this is serious.'

They moved to the back utility room to talk without waking the others. Ken was leaning against their 16-foot chest freezer, its red power light visible in the dark, the compressor humming softly. He confessed that he was at wit's end.

"Why?" Ken asked. "Why are you constantly running away?"

"I don't know," Clarence said.

Clarence recalls the moment after his response:

> Ken was crying. And I had never seen that. He was such a strong, silent man. You could see he loved me. He was trying to do something. He was trying to reach me. He was trying to connect with me, to the best that he could. It was one of those moments where our spirits connected. I felt bad, embarrassed that I would make him cry.

However, Clarence couldn't explain himself:

> I didn't have my voice. I couldn't talk about things because I didn't know why I was doing the things I was doing. I was just doing them.

In the end, after their emotional conversation, Clarence apologized and said that he'd try harder. They hugged and he walked upstairs. Reflecting back on that time in his life now, Clarence provides more insight:

> I think that just knowing that I wasn't a part of their family. And when you're always being introduced as a foster child, that's who you are. It feels like you're never good enough to make that cut, to be part of the family.

Despite their heart-to-heart, the relationship between Clarence and his foster father did not improve significantly.

> I think it was that conversation that sparked them to start thinking about what they could do to stop me from running away.

It wasn't long after their chat that Ken decided it would be a good idea to purchase Clarence a snowmobile. They found a used one for sale — a 340cc Ski-Doo, called The Silver Bullet.

> I was all proud; all my friends had one. I got a helmet and a Ski-Doo suit. Then the first or second time I had it out, I was riding through some drifts beside some evergreen trees we planted. I gave 'er, went over the drift and it shot me right into the evergreens. I scraped the hood and broke the windshield.

Clarence has a distinct memory of Ken taking the snowmobile out for rides, wearing his big black Wellington boots; he "looked really funny: a farmer on a snowmobile." However, despite the Reiers' gifts, Clarence never did stay for too long when he was back at the farm.

> It was me having this identity crisis, having no sense of belonging, having abandonment issues, and not knowing all these 'whys.' And then having intergenerational trauma in my blood from generation to generation to generation.

Over time, Clarence's time away from the farm started to increase. He would move around in a transient state from one home to another, until eventually he wore out his welcome. It was at this time that he experienced his first episode of alcohol poisoning. "It was moonshine or something like that," he recalls, mentioning that he slept for three days straight. It was also around this time, in the winter of 1980-81, that he committed an armed robbery. Fortunately, no one was hurt.

> It was a gradual progression that led up to that incident. It was a state of hopelessness, where I didn't care, I didn't have feelings for anybody else, let alone myself. I think I was just so disconnected, and I was looking for belonging in the group that I was hanging out with.

Although he wasn't caught at first, he had other interactions with police throughout that winter, which eventually led to a new group home.

> On Madison Street, just half-way up the hill, there was a house there called Madison House. It was like a group home/detention centre.

Unlike other group homes, Clarence grew relatively content

living in this one. He connected with one of the social workers and became friends with many of the other youth in the home. That spring (1981) a detective came to visit him.

> They wanted me to confess to the robbery because it was an unsolved case. They said all they wanted me to do was admit to it and then they could close the case, so I did.

Because Clarence was just under sixteen years old, he wasn't charged. Instead, he remained at Madison House where he recalls with fondness various activities:

> We'd go on fishing trips. We'd do outings. We'd get some money. We'd hang out downtown and we'd go to the arcades because Kitchener had a bunch of arcades back in the day.
>
> There were boys there. There were girls there. And I can remember we'd sneak through the second storey windows. The boys' and girls' dormitories were side by side. At night time you could sneak out one window from the boys' side and go into the girls' side and do whatever boys and girls do.

At the end of the summer, Clarence was kicked out of the group home after he came home past the curfew one too many times. Staff told him that he had to leave.

> I got so fricken' angry because I was having a good time there. It was a good memorable summer.

After a brief visit back at the Reiers, he once again ran away. Within weeks, he was taken into police custody for a string of break-and-enters along Queen Street in downtown Kitchener.

I don't know why I did those. It was just stupid. But when I did get caught, I went into a group home again outside of Kitchener.

This was the second time he had stayed at this particular home, and now he had to go back to school at Eastwood Collegiate for grade eleven. However, after a couple weeks, in September of 1981, Clarence turned sixteen years old and withdrew from school. CAS records report that around this time Clarence began living on his own at various addresses.

There is a well-to-do neighbourhood in the south end of downtown Kitchener called Rockway Gardens. Enjoying his newfound freedom, Clarence was out late with two of his friends roaming the wealthy neighbourhood one cold winter night. They decided to break into an especially nice house they saw, hoping to find valuables to quickly sell at pawn shops. As one would expect, the spontaneous break-in was not well-planned by the daring teenagers.

The house was a small bungalow, backing onto a golf course, off Courtland Street near Ottawa Street. Once inside, they began rummaging through the house in the dark but Clarence recalls that they suddenly heard a vehicle pull into the driveway. As the teenagers scrambled to leave, they knocked loose the old skeleton key that was in the front door, which prevented them from opening it. The back door opened and two people stepped inside. Clarence and his friends held their breath. There was no escape. They heard someone say, "I think they're still in the house."

When the lights turned on, two senior homeowners discovered that they were unwitting hosts to three guests. Clarence and his crew quickly ran past the startled couple, who promptly called the police. Clarence recalls what happened next:

We all ran in different directions. About a block away there was a run-down apartment building, on Ottawa Street. I ran in there because I was familiar with that apartment building; I knew a guy who lived upstairs.

> I ran into the basement and tried to hide. I heard the police come in because they were canvassing the area. I heard them knock on an apartment door and asked if they had heard or seen anything. Someone said, 'I haven't seen anybody, but I heard someone run in here.' Then they found me hiding out in the basement.

He was brought to the police station and while in custody an officer asked if he was aware whose house they broke into. No, he wasn't. The officer said, "you were lucky that their son wasn't with them, because he's a professional hockey player and if he would've been there, there would have been no need to call us." After an intimidating interview, Clarence admitted to being involved in the break-ins along Queen Street.

> Then I went to a different group home. It was a gated-community kind of group home.

On November 25, 1981, now sixteen years old, Clarence was sentenced to six months at Burtch Correctional Facility, which is closed now but was in Brant County, south of Waterloo Region.[2]

> I remember walking into Burtch and doing an intake. They take all your city clothes off of you and then they give you your blue clothes... I remember walking into this open dorm and there was a guy lying on the bed. He looked right at me and just spit on the floor, and then he just stared at me as I walked by and found my bed. And I'm going: Oh fuck, this is not going to be good.

After he was organized into a range, Clarence befriended an older man named Al who was from Hamilton. Al took him under his wing and taught him how to survive in jail.

> He was a short, stocky guy, tattoos. He taught me that you can learn a lot from just watching people; he taught me not to ask a lot of questions, to keep my mouth shut. He taught me to not get involved — 'just mind your own business and do your own time.'

Life at Burtch followed a daily routine. Clarence was assigned kitchen chores at a cannery on the premises. He would have to clean up after shifts in the afternoon and evening. There were movie nights in a big barn on the property. Eileen, Ken, and Keith often came to visit him; "I was thankful for their company, but I also felt shameful," he recalls. The Reiers suggested that after being released he should return to the farm to live and work there. Clarence did apply for an early release, but the wardens and officers judged him unlikely to stay out of trouble.

> When I went up it was always 'nay.' But probably for good reason. I was high-risk. I was young.

After four months in jail, on January 25, 1982, Clarence gave Al a hug and was released with a one-year probation order. He moved back to the farm in New Dundee.

Clarence spent the rest of the winter at the Reiers' farm. When the weather warmed in the spring of April 1982, once again Clarence could not resist the freedom of life on his own. As he had many times before, he made his way to one of the arcades in downtown Kitchener where he could reliably find friends from the city. It was there that he met up with a group he knew from his time spent in the youth detention centre.

> We figured out how to get the money and we all went down to Toronto, which was a pretty wild experience because I didn't know Toronto. These friends of mine said they'd been there before so I just took their

word and they said we'd be okay and we'd all stick
together as a crew, as a little posse, right?

The four of them took a bus to the big city. After arriving, for
the first couple nights, the crew of teenagers stayed at the Greyhound bus shelter. They were always harassed by security guards.
Despite their intention to stick together, eventually the friends
went their separate ways, each on their own adventure.

Alone in the sprawling Toronto metropolis, Clarence suddenly
found himself in difficult straits. After a few nights sleeping in the
bus terminal, he discovered a youth shelter to stay in. "I was never
so happy to go stay in a shelter," he recalls. He made some friends
there, but it wasn't long before he was kicked out, likely for
breaking the curfew, but he doesn't remember exactly why.

> There was a lot of stuff going on back then in
> Toronto. I don't think it was safe for young people to
> be around back then.

Soon after being banned from the shelter, Clarence ran out of
money. He realized that he was completely isolated in a city of
millions of unfamiliar people. Without shelter, without cash,
without friends, Clarence suddenly found himself homeless in
Toronto and struggling to survive.

"I had to resort to male prostitution to survive," Clarence says,
explaining that he was familiar with the idea because he had heard
of other friends doing something similar when they needed money.
He made his way to a small, pornographic movie theatre downtown. He doesn't remember paying for a ticket, but it seemed that
the theatre staff did not care that minors were on the premises. It
was outside this theatre that men propositioned Clarence for
sexual acts.

> I can remember these older men asking me and
> picking me up and taking me somewhere either in

their car or back to their apartment. And one guy was playing pornos. He had an old movie projector, and he was playing pornos — while he was abusing me. And, and then he'd give me some money at the time too. And that happened on and off I'd say maybe three times in Toronto.

It brought me a lot of shame. It brought me a lot of confusion. It brought me a lot of the 'why?' Why did I let that happen? Why did it happen to me? Why did they pick me? It was something I didn't want anybody to know about.

After these traumatic experiences, Clarence's memory of the rest of his time in Toronto is disjointed. At some point a friend introduced him to a man who had an apartment downtown Toronto.

It was probably around that time that I met this guy who was a professional referee for soccer games. He was gay and he let me stay in his apartment. He would take me to his soccer games and let me crash at his place. He'd buy me shoes and pick me up stuff.

The man let Clarence stay at his place for a few days and even found him some paid work at a car wash nearby. He seemed to be a resource for street-involved youth.

He never did come on to me, but in reflection, his friendship and affection was most likely a form of grooming. I think I was intuitively figuring that out at the time.

Clarence also remembers one night partying with other kids and using diazepam, commonly known as Valium.

> We took a big jar from this guy who was selling pills
> on the street. I remember we just swarmed him and
> took the jar from him. We took a couple of pills,
> didn't feel anything, took a couple more, and then we
> went for a subway ride. I heard from my friends later
> that I fell asleep on the subway and they couldn't
> wake me up.

His friends took him to Women's College Hospital and
dropped him off there.

> I remember waking up in intensive care. I was in a
> bed in a room. I had an IV; it was dark, night-time. I
> didn't know where I was; I started panicking a bit
> and pulled the intravenous out of my arm. I found
> my clothes and took off, found some steps — because
> I was hungry, I was starving — found some steps and
> I went down a couple flights and I found a fridge.

After eating some food, Clarence left the hospital, making his
way back to the streets.

Another memory of his time in Toronto involves being inter-
viewed in a city park by a news anchor for CityTV. The news crew
was filming a segment on juveniles living on the street. He and his
friend both gave their input on the issue, excited to be featured on
local news.

As to how Clarence finally ended up coming home, there are
two different explanations. According to Clarence's memory, he
was visiting the Eaton Centre shopping mall when police recognized him from the local news. They asked his name and discovered that he was in breach of probation. However, according to
CAS records, Clarence was discovered in Toronto after ending up
in the hospital for a severe asthma attack.

Whatever happened, Clarence knows for sure that in the end
he was brought home in the backseat of a Waterloo police cruiser,

after roughly two weeks of survival in the city. Although he had no belongings, riding in the backseat of that police cruiser, Clarence carried back home something that would stay with him for the rest of his life, a powerful secret.

 That was a time of confusion, of vulnerability. That was a time when I experienced trauma and almost died with that overdose. And reflecting back, I'm probably very lucky because it could've ended up a lot worse than it did. When I reflect back on that time, there's a memory: it's like there's a cloud or a mist around there and I can't see clearly. Certain parts are still buried or are gone. I think that's my mind protecting me — I'm not really sure. I know I was looking for something but what I found was not what I was looking for. That's for sure. That time in Toronto stayed with me for a long time. It wasn't until I was forty-five years old when I was finally able to start disclosing that time in my life.

I didn't want anybody to know about my time in Toronto or about what happened to me, because I thought I would be judged. I thought I would be stereotyped. I thought I would be made fun of. So I took those times and I buried them deep inside of me for a very long time.

6

NEW RELATIONSHIPS

I n late April 1982, Clarence left Toronto and went back to the Reiers' to live and work on the farm.

> It was very structured living. I had to get up, I had to do chores. I had responsibilities. Every third Sunday it was my job to do the chores, which was challenging. I forget what they were paying me.

By now, some of his friends had driver's licenses, so it was simpler to get together. Stephanie was one of those friends and they soon started dating again, in spite of Clarence's absences.

On the weekends Clarence would visit and stay with his friends in the city, attending parties, going for swims in nearby lakes, or weekend camping trips. Stephanie didn't live too far away, about a ten-minute drive or half an hour on a bicycle. At this point, Cheryl was no longer living at the farm. She lived in Kitchener, but came to visit, and Clarence would also see her when he was in the city.

After three months back on the farm, the Barton's Inn, a hotel in downtown New Dundee burnt down. Soon after on a weekend,

Clarence was hanging out with his longtime buddies from elementary school. It dawned on them that there would probably still be alcohol in the fridges of the burnt-out hotel. All they had to do was successfully navigate its charred remains.

> Thank goodness we didn't get killed and the thing didn't collapse on us or beams fall on us. But, yeah, we made it into where the coolers were, opened them up and, yeah, it was full of beer, full of quarts, big quarts of Labatt's Blue. And we pulled a bunch out and we sat there and drank them.

Puffed up on alcohol, the three friends decided to break into a convenience store. The crime was reported in the morning, and it wasn't difficult for the police to locate the culprits in such a small town. Breaking and entering combined with a breach of probation meant that Clarence was sentenced to prison once again, this time for one year at Mimico Correctional Centre in Toronto.

> I learned a lot in jail. I never got beat up in jail or stabbed or abused, but I learned some lessons: that you could really tell a lot by just watching someone — observe them; see how they treat people; and that will give you a good definition of who they are and what their character is like.

Clarence started a "two-for-one" business in his area of the prison. He would lend items to jail-mates who were expected to return two of the same after Canteen day. There was also a mattress factory run out of the prison where Clarence found full-time work. He managed to save up a little money.

While he was in prison, Stephanie wrote letters to Clarence, which he says had quite an impact on him:

> I couldn't believe that she would want to show interest in me, for somebody who's in jail, right?... I guess she always believed in me. I guess she always had thoughts that maybe I would change.

The Reiers came to visit every now and then, mainly Ken and Keith. Clarence also received an unexpected visit from a family friend, a man who had gotten to know Clarence through church.

> It made me feel good that someone cared who wasn't family. He even talked to me about my parents.

Cheryl also came to visit him often. She was living in Toronto at the time. "She was always there to support me," says Clarence. He remembers that he was even granted a leave for the Christmas holidays and he and Cheryl drove up to the Reiers' to stay with the family.

By law, most people who are sentenced to prison only serve two thirds of their time before being released to spend the remainder under supervision. Clarence avoided getting into fights or dealing drugs — for the most part. He did get caught twice smoking weed, for which he was placed in segregation and given an extra month on his sentence.

> I guess the only positive thing about being thrown in the hole is I learned to play cribbage. There was a guy also in there who taught me how to play.

At 12:01 a.m. on March 28, 1983, seventeen-year-old Clarence was released from Mimico, his second stint in prison, with a backpack and over a thousand dollars cash in hand (his savings from work at the mattress factory). He took a taxi to the nearest motel but was refused a room. He managed to find a place to stay that night in a bed and breakfast. The next day he went shopping downtown Toronto at the Eaton Centre and bought himself a leather jacket. Then he took a bus back to Kitchener, where one of the Reiers picked him up and brought him to the farm. The Reiers had already informed Clarence that he would be welcome back once he was out.

Things went well on the farm for a few months. Clarence and Stephanie continued their relationship. He started to take on more responsibilities, sometimes tending to the pigs over the weekend when the Reiers went away.

> The strained relationship with the Reiers was starting to repair itself. I was starting to have a better understanding of them and how they were there to support me and to love me to the best of their abilities.

But one of those weekends when the Reiers were away things got a little out of hand. Clarence invited a few friends over. They started to party, which included taking some of the farm vehicles out for a joyride. In the morning, the yard was a mess, strewn about with the farm implements. Clarence's foster brother Keith came over — he lived in a house on an adjacent property — and knocked on the door to see what was going on.

> I can remember hiding in the house because I knew it was my brother and that I was in shit. Right after he left, I just left.

This was the last time Clarence ran away from the farm.[1]

CLARENCE'S SISTER Cheryl let him stay at her place until he found a room for rent with close friends. Soon he found a job at a mattress factory called Waterloo Bedding. Ironically, his job was to monitor machines that produced fire-retardant foam that would be installed in mattresses destined for prison cells.

> I lasted there maybe six to eight months, maybe a year. It was an old two-storey building — right where the parking lot for Vincenzo's is... I'd always party and not show up for work. The boss came to my door and banged on the door. He knew where I was living and he'd come and bang on the door, trying to get me to come to work. I can remember hiding and not going and seeing him. I don't think I got fired from there; I just never went back.

In the meantime, Clarence's use of drugs and alcohol was becoming increasingly reckless. One incident was quite unbelievable. High on LSD, Clarence took his girlfriend's parents' car out for a drive, without their knowing. He and a friend went to New Dundee to pick up some beer at his friend's place. On their way back, they tried to evade a police cruiser that had started to tail them. They were not able to flee, and eventually Clarence pulled over, thinking it was better to stop before something worse happened. The officer asked for his license and registration. Clarence had neither.

> And then I was arrested. They threw me in the car. Yeah. Towed the car and — fuck — it was a bad scene.

He was charged with driving under the influence and escape by flight. On top of that, his rocky relationship with Stephanie's parents — high school dropout, criminal record — spiralled to a new low. "That kind of put a stop on our dating for a while," Clarence admits. Fortunately, Stephanie's parents decided not to press any charges, so Clarence only received an extension on his probation order.

However, besides a few notable blips, over the next couple of years, Clarence maintained steady work in Kitchener with stable living conditions and he and Stephanie developed an increasingly serious relationship. One of their favourite activities was going on camping trips during the humid Ontario summers. But life as Clarence knew it suddenly changed one Saturday night in the winter of 1985.

Camping at Pinery Provincial Park, Grand Bend, Ontario

At the age of twenty-one, he got an unexpected phone call from Cheryl.

66 She said, "Hey bro, what are you doing?"
I said, "It's Saturday night. What do you think I'm doing? I'm partying at Debbie and Jerry's."
She says, "I got something to tell you. And I'm

bringing somebody over to see you, within twenty minutes to half an hour."

And I go, "What do you mean? Who are you bringing over?"

And she says, "I'm bringing over our father."

And I went, "Yeah right."

She goes, "No I'm serious. Our dad is standing right in front of me."

7

THE SCHOOLS

> I carry the Copper Cup to acknowledge the proper-
> ties of water. Water is life and water is sacred. I also
> carry the Cup to acknowledge the importance of
> women, and how we always need that feminine part
> to accompany the masculine, to have unity and
> balance in our lives. We are all connected to our
> grandmothers.

In the early 1900s, Clarence's great grandparents, Charles Saylors — son of Mary McLeod and Isaiah Saylors — and his wife Helen, lived in the town of Chapleau. When the First World War started, Charles enlisted in the army and was deployed overseas. While fighting, he was exposed to chemical weapons and developed lung issues that persisted after he returned to Chapleau. Charles managed to survive for several years with the help of Cree medicines. During this time his wife Helen passed away, leaving him with their three daughters. To help Charles manage, his father Isaiah agreed to take care of the youngest. But a few years later, Charles succumbed to his lung issues and passed away. The two eldest daughters, Margaret and Hannah, were both taken into St

John's Indian Residential School. It was March, 1924, when Margaret Saylors, four years old at the time, entered St John's Indian Residential School in Chapleau, Ontario. She was the first of Clarence's ancestors to enter Canada's residential school system.

Indian Residential Schools in Canada have roots reaching as far back as the early 1600s, when Roman Catholic missionaries established boarding schools in New France, which the French Empire was slowly colonising with permanent settlements. Catholic missionaries from France came to North America seeking to convert Indigenous Peoples to the Christian faith. The missionaries lived among Indigenous Peoples, learned their languages and culture, constructed chapels, and eventually helped establish smaller settlements. Their missionary work progressed slowly. One small part of the mission work was boarding schools that sought to use education to convert Indigenous children and assimilate them into Western-European culture. However, Indigenous Peoples had a particularly strong negative reaction to boarding schools that took children away from their families and communities; they resisted these misguided efforts to convert Indigenous children. Nonetheless, European missionaries persisted in removing Indigenous children from the influence of their culture, and these boarding school experiments continued over the centuries.

By 1847, when the settlement and colonization of the land that would soon be known as Canada was in full swing, Egerton Ryerson, Chief Superintendent of Education for Upper Canada (Ontario), proposed that the British colonial government establish "industrial schools" with "domestic and religious education" for Indigenous children. Bolstered by the racist ideology of white supremacy — the lie that humans belong to naturally ranked biological races, with white Europeans conveniently located at the top — Ryerson mistakenly believed that First Nations were an inferior civilization in need of purportedly benevolent help from Christian-European colonizers for their survival and salvation. Like early Catholic efforts, the industrial schools failed to achieve their purposes. According to those in charge, the reason that the schools were not able to Christianize and assimilate children were due to a series of factors: the students were enrolled at a late age, parents of children were not convinced of the schools' usefulness, and insufficient funding from the government.

When Canada became a nation in 1867, the newly formed government made a promise to Britain that it would continue to uphold treaty obligations with Indigenous Peoples previously established during the past centuries of trade and colonization. But Canada was a settler colonial state anxious for control of land and access to the land's resources. With outright warfare outlawed (and evidently costly, based on the experience of the United States south of the border), the government instead pursued a project of cultural genocide.[1] One way to avoid having to honour treaty obligations was to erase the existence of Indigenous Peoples as such. Canada implemented a series of policies and actions to this effect, and its "Indian Residential School System" became one of the main tools for this crime against humanity.

In 1879, after researching boarding schools in the United States and the Canadian West, John A. MacDonald, then prime minister of Canada, acted on recommendations to use both Christianity and education as a tool to force Indigenous Peoples' assimilation into mainstream society, attempting to solve the government's so-called "Indian problem." Disrupting the transmission of culture to children is an effective way to ensure its future destruction. The dominant religious orders in Canada — including Roman Catholic, Anglican, Methodist, United, and Presbyterian churches — proved convenient and willing partners for establishing and running the schools. Indeed, the churches had already built schools and many of them were staffed voluntarily by devout missionaries.

Christians viewed — and many continue to do so — Indigenous religions as pagan and evil, but mass conversions of Indigenous Peoples had had limited success. Church organizations partnered with the government to increase conversion efforts, in part because it afforded them an opportunity to convert youth into their religious communities. As a result, school staff considered their work humanitarian in nature.

In 1886, the Canadian government amended the Indian Act, making it mandatory for Indigenous children between the ages six and fifteen to attend residential schools and granting "truancy officers" the power to forcibly remove children from the homes of unwilling parents. Guiding this new policy was the notion that "aggressive civilizing" would only be effective if children were completely cut off from contact with their parents and their Indigenous cultures at a young age. In the same vein, residential school policy sought to stifle cultural expression by prohibiting students from speaking their Indigenous languages, having prolonged visits with family, and practicing traditional ceremonies. This is how the schools became an extension of the government's larger agenda of assimilating Indigenous identities into mainstream society (and thereby extinguishing their treaty rights and the government's treaty responsibilities).

Indigenous parents were generally not supportive of the schools. But as European colonization and settler encroachment onto their territory intensified, they were increasingly forced to seek ways to adapt to their new environment. For some, European education seemed to provide a promising path forward for the children. Nonetheless, whether they believed this or not, the Indian Act made it punishable by law for parents to withhold their children from residential schooling.

From the beginning, residential schools were chronically underfunded, which had a series of consequences. The school's curriculum typically followed a half-day system, which involved having the children spend part of each day in studies and the other part working to support the institution. Under the guise of vocational training, schools often put children to work in laborious activities meant to generate revenue, such as farming or manufacturing. When students were actually in the classroom, the curriculum often emphasized religious instruction — the school principals considered the primary goal of the institution to be converting the students to Christian beliefs (which aligned with the government's agenda to erase Indigenous identities). Similarly, the so-called vocational training was intended to replace traditional living skills with industrial labour skills.

Underfunded and poorly maintained, the schools caused the students to suffer beyond the trauma of being taken from their families because their basic physical needs were not met. Shoddy construction and lack of repairs led to sanitary and safety issues. In the wintertime, the uninsulated buildings were not adequately heated. Broken plumbing caused damp and moldy conditions, and cockroaches were almost always present, often spoiling food stores. Food quality varied between the schools, but it was usually poor.

Living in a poorly-ventilated building, lacking nutritious food, and under stressful psychological conditions, the students were very vulnerable to disease. During the early years of residential schooling, Duncan Campbell Scott, deputy minister of Indian Affairs at the time, estimated that nearly fifty percent of the children enrolled died before graduating. The exact numbers are impossible to know because neither the government nor the churches kept detailed records of student deaths, and students who died were often buried in unmarked graves. Canada's Truth and Reconciliation Commission (2015) found reports of 3,201 student deaths between 1867-2000, noting that the true number is likely much higher due to poor record-keeping.[2] In 2021, an anthropologist discovered evidence of approximately 200 unmarked graves at Kamloops Indian Residential School in British Columbia, and since then evidence of unmarked graves at several additional sites has been discovered on the former grounds of residential schools across Canada.

In addition to physical suffering, the students also experienced psychological and emotional abuse that exacerbated the damage done by being torn from their families and culture. Teachers taught the students to disdain their ethnic identities and punished them for speaking their native languages. They also taught that the students' traditional spirituality and ceremonies were evil. Parents of students were surprised to find their children disdainful and untrusting of the family when they returned home. Many children had been brainwashed to despise their own heritage. Upon entering the schools, the students were assigned an identification number that staff often used in place of names. Punishment for breaking the rules — such as speaking to a classmate in Cree instead of English — might involve public humiliation, physical reprimand, or forced isolation. Up until the 1950s, there were very few qualified teachers at the schools. In part, this was because residential schools paid less than public schools in urban centres and were usually located in isolated areas. The teachers and staff who ended up at the schools were often those who could not attain work elsewhere or who had been fired for misconduct. There were always high turnover rates. Underfunded, the schools also lacked oversight from the federal administrators of the program.

One especially appalling harm of the schools was the many cases of students who were sexually abused by school staff. Rarely were these incidents prosecuted. More often student (or parent) accusations were ignored by the administration. If there was an investigation, it was kept internal and usually went no further than an inquiry when the person accused would simply deny the accusation. When the abuse was too obvious to ignore — for instance, when another staff member witnessed it — school administration or government officials would almost always dismiss the staff without involving the police. Rather than address the problem and hold offenders accountable, school authorities sought to cover up the incident to protect the reputation of the church and the government. As a result, many students left the schools harbouring the trauma of childhood sexual abuse.

Vulnerable children enduring psychological, emotional, and

physical abuse are forced to find ways to cope and survive. Many were hardened to the world around them and lacking role models or social support, they lashed out at their peers. Bullying others is one way to seek control in an unpredictable and unforgiving environment. It feels empowering to demean others; and it can also help conceal one's own feeling of vulnerability. The prevalence of bullying was often made worse by the fact that there was a general lack of supervision at the schools caused by underfunding and a lack of empathy for suffering.

Although the purposes of the schools were certainly destructive, not all student experiences were fully negative, and many students developed and demonstrated incredible resilience. Some of the teachers who taught at the schools deeply believed that they were doing the right thing and treated their charges with kindness and respect as best they could. While in a significant minority, these teachers are remembered fondly by alumni for their dedication and empathy. Some graduates went on to pursue higher education and/or become leaders in their communities. However, the existence of some positive experiences does not absolve the system from its undeniably destructive intentions and effects. The vast majority of students did not fare well. They left with very few life skills, confused about their identity, harbouring severe trauma, and lacking an emotional connection to their family and culture. Parents and grandparents were likewise disconnected as their children returned home lacking language skills and dismissive of their culture. Many children felt as if they belonged neither in their home communities nor in settler society. This alienation from family and culture had serious ripple effects. The Survivors of the schools never had the opportunity to learn important life skills from their home communities, such as good parenting. They often weren't able to cope with raising their own families. Many turned to drugs and alcohol to help them cope with life after school.

The Chapleau Indian Boarding School, located on the outskirts of the town of Chapleau and operated by the Anglican Diocese of Moosonee, first opened its doors in January 1907. It was a large building with a capacity for roughly forty children. A couple years after opening, the church signed an operational agreement with the federal government that officially made the school a part of Canada's residential school system. By 1920, the school was rebuilt in a new location just outside of town and renamed St John's Anglican Indian Residential School.

During the 1920s, parents of children enrolled in St John's Residential School began to protest in Chapleau. They charged, among other things, that students at the school were being treated with undue cruelty and were receiving an inadequate education. The government arranged an investigation: in the final report, the investigator, a lawyer named A. G. Chisholm, concluded that "not more than eight hours weekly is devoted to study... The balance of the weekly period at the Chapleau school is for the boys, spent in hard, grinding labour, or in the case of the girls, at scrubbing, cleaning, and other domestic duties."[3]

Margaret Saylors at St John's Residential School third from left, c. 1933

Margaret Saylors was at St John's Residential School during the parent protests. In total, she spent twelve years in the institution. On June 30, 1936, she graduated and left the school grounds, sixteen years old. Later, she met Howard Cachagee, who was also

Chapleau Cree, and they began a relationship. In time, they were married and had five children: Charles, Michael, James, Clarence (Abby), Marjorie, and Ernest. The fourth child, Clarence Hubert Cachagee, was born in 1943. He would become the father of Clarence Michael Cachagee.

Margaret Saylors and Howard Cachagee, c.1940

Abby Cachagee (1991)

Everything was so quiet. I could hear things that I'd never heard before. The sky was clear. And then out of the east there appeared this big crow. Circled me and circled me three times and then he took off to the south and disappeared. And I went back.

And he says, "Well, what did you do?"
"I didn't pray so much," I said. "I just looked around and listened."
He says, "What did you see?"
And I says, "I seen —" I told him what I had seen.
And then he says, "Well." He says, "your relatives now have started to come back and look at you." And he says, "What type of bird was it?"
And I says, "It was a crow."
He says, "Your name is Cachagee (Cackachew) and" — he says — "in Cree that means crow. There's relationship between that."
And he says, "From now on wherever you go there will be crows around you and with you."

8

FROM ONE FAMILY TO FOUR

It was totally unexpected, the phone call Clarence received from his sister in the winter of 1985 announcing that his biological father had appeared. Clarence remembers his reaction:

> A whole wave, flood of emotions washed over me. I probably almost fainted. I think I was speechless because something that I wanted for so long in my entire life was there in front of me. I was scared. I was happy. I was angry. I was confused.

After Cheryl hung up, Clarence called his foster father, Ken. "Dad, what do I do?" he asked.

Ken told him that Clarence knew what to do, that he needed to meet his father. Clarence must have been in a state of shock because he doesn't now remember this conversation. It was his foster-brother Keith who reminded him that it had happened, years later.

Before long, there was a knock at the door. In came Cheryl and with her a tall man, long hair down to the middle of his back. He introduced himself as Abby Cachagee. It was obvious to both

Clarence and Cheryl that he was their father. After a moment of silence Clarence spoke up: "I don't know whether to hug you or to punch you, because it's fine that you're here now but where were you all those years?"

Abby apologized for his absence. He said that he had a lot of explaining to do and that he would never leave them again.

Soon after that initial meeting, Abby contacted Maureen, Clarence's mother, who had since remarried, and in a matter of weeks Abby was taking Clarence and Cheryl to meet her in Toronto.

> Maureen was like ninety pounds soaking wet, just this small woman, right? I'm thinking, 'Wow, you're my mom?' It was cool. It was strange. How do you act? How do you receive something that's never been there? How do you have that bond? So it was really awkward at first. It was kind of very exciting and overwhelming, but it was also awkward.

During the next few weeks, Clarence and Cheryl met all sorts of extended family: cousins, uncles, aunts.

> We were like the lost children, the lost souls who got reunited with the family, which was strange at times.

Despite how surreal it all felt, Clarence got along well with his newly discovered family. They were very accepting of him.

> I think some people warned us to just slow things down a bit, because it might be too overwhelming for Cheryl and I. It might be too overwhelming for my dad or my mom, because they already had their own lives that they were living for such a long time and all of a sudden we pop in and we're adults.

At the time of their introduction, Clarence's father was living in a semi-detached home in downtown Toronto. He was working for the federal government in the immigration services department. A few months after they met, Clarence moved in with his father, while Cheryl went to live with Maureen. Clarence's partner Stephanie also moved to Toronto, living with her brother who happened to live in the same neighbourhood as Maureen.

Clarence and Abby got along quite well.

> He was a good guy. He was kind. He was soft. He was gentle. He was patient. He always thought before he spoke. He was witty. He was a good man.

While living with Abby in Toronto, Clarence found work with a cousin who managed a sprinkler-fitting business in the city. Clarence usually rode the bus for an hour or so to get to wherever he was working that day. He was making it work, but the living conditions in Abby's house were not great. Clarence remembers one summer night that turned sleepless when he felt something scurry over his exposed body, a cockroach.

> Freaked me right out. I'd never seen or been exposed to anything like that in my life until I went to Toronto.

This whole living situation was quite an unforeseen development in Clarence's life. Only one month earlier, he was living in Kitchener oblivious to the existence of his biological parents and extended family. Now he was getting to know a whole family he never knew he had and living and working in a new big city. As Clarence built relationships with his new family, Abby began to explain to Clarence his Cree heritage. He taught him how to smudge, how to pray and cleanse oneself with the smoke of burning sage.

Visit to Fox Lake Reserve

I can remember Abby taking us up to the reserve. I think that was just when Fox Lake was relocated. The first time I went up there, our band office was voting out of a trailer. But I got to meet my uncles and my cousins and my aunts. And I got to know that I come from a really big family and that we have some lineage and some history that goes back quite a ways.

That was my first introduction to being who I truly was as an Original Person of this land, to having that connection. I think that ignited a flame inside of me. It started something burning. But because I was under the influence and my dad was under the influence, there were only so many things that I could be exposed to.

Clarence learned that Abby "loved to stir the pot" when Abby told him that he was once arrested at Fox Lake Reserve for raising hell over politics he disagreed with. As Clarence got to know his father, it became clear to him that Abby also had inner struggles. Although he rarely went into detail about his childhood experiences, he did disclose to Clarence that he was a Survivor of Canada's residential school system. Clarence reflects:

> I cannot imagine what life would be like after coming out of the Indian Residential School System. I cannot imagine the horrendous conditions that he lived through, the abuse that he suffered, the abuse that he witnessed. And then to still try to live life and come back into a community or a family after you've been disconnected or displaced from them and everything else, for maybe over ten years of your life growing up. It makes total sense to me why so many individuals turn to drugs and alcohol to cope with the traumas that they experienced while they were in those schools.
>
> Alcohol, for me, took away the shame, the confusion, the anger, the abandonment issues, the 'whys'. It washed all of that away for short periods of time. Whenever I was in trouble with the law, alcohol was a common thread. Alcohol was always a contributing factor for my father to escape. I can't imagine what he went through growing up, in those residential schools, and then after leaving those schools and trying to find his identity.

Clarence recounts one surprising story Abby told him. It started when Abby had come across an employment ad in the newspaper calling for Indigenous actors. A film production company was shooting a movie in England — it turned out to be the film *Revolution*, starring Al Pacino — and they needed extras for the set. Abby had never acted before, but he jumped at the opportunity and his application was approved. He went to

England and worked on the movie set. Unfortunately, however, like Clarence, Abby also used substances to cope with underlying issues. He had to return to Canada before the filming was finished.

But Clarence explains that, in fact, Abby very rarely drank alcohol.

> [Abby] was a chronic cannabis smoker and he struggled not to drink alcohol. Out of the eighteen years that I knew him, I think he only drank five times.

Clarence and Abby's lifestyles worked well together; as Clarence puts it: "It was like two peas in a pod."

Clarence also attributes both his own and his father's substance use as a barrier to reconnecting with their culture, explaining:

> Because I was under the influence too, I really couldn't experience and absorb the teachings like one could with a sober mind, to be connected, to be mindful, to be aware.

After six months of living with Abby, Clarence moved in with his mother, Maureen. He had been living with his father in an effort to get to know him but also wanted to spend time with his mother. Because the living situation with his dad wasn't great, it felt like the right time to make the move.

> My mom was a very kind woman. She was a hard worker. She'd get up and go to work every day. She worked in a wallpaper factory. She worked there for years and years and years.

As Maureen and Clarence got to know each other, they started to feel like family: "You could tell that she really tried her best to show affection because she did love us."

Maureen took Clarence and Cheryl up north to the city in which she was born, North Bay, so that they could meet her side of the family, who were descendants of Scottish and Irish settlers. Clarence felt good meeting all his relatives. They were a tight-knit family. As he met both sides of his family, Clarence recalls:

> That was the beginning of Cheryl and I knowing what it's like to have a family, to come from our family, to know who our parents are, to have a sense of belonging, a connection. And then that's when everything started to make sense of why we were exposed to what we were exposed to when we were young.

Maureen spoke little of the circumstances around Cheryl's and Clarence's births. However, she did explain how she had tried to take care of her children, seeking arrangements with other family members in North Bay or Kitchener. But like Abby, Maureen also struggled with substance use and, as a result, could not provide stable living conditions for her children. When Clarence speaks about substance use, he says:

> You could see that on both sides of the family addiction was there, alcohol and drugs were there — probably to mask the pain, or to help people cope with some of the traumas or experiences that they faced in their own lives.

Although Maureen did not share with Clarence many details about the circumstances of his early years with her, family memories and CAS records shed light on the extraordinary challenges that she faced as a young mother.

In March 1963, Maureen and Abby were married in Callander, Ontario. They moved to Kitchener together but soon afterwards, Abby was incarcerated for car theft. Maureen then moved back to Callander, finding a living arrangement with her grandparents. Her own parents were not able or willing to provide support. She gave birth to Cheryl in late 1963; Maureen was sixteen years old at the time. When Clarence was born two years later, Maureen was temporarily in Kitchener seeking employment opportunities. Abby was in and out of the picture throughout this time — he was trying to support the family but was not able to stay out of trouble with the law.

Things took a turn for the worse in August of 1966. Maureen's grandfather retired the month before and was no longer able to support her and her children. She moved with her children to Kitchener to look for stable work. At the same time, Abby admitted himself into a hospital in North Bay, after an episode that involved the police while he was in "a severe state of depression." Over the next two months, Maureen struggled immensely to find work and take care of the children. She experienced health issues which made matters worse. On November 1, Maureen met with a CAS social worker, asking for money to help pay for childcare. The social worker provided some money and offered temporary wardship at this time. Two days later, Abby was incarcerated again for driving without a licence. The following day Maureen agreed to hand over her children to CAS. Letters in CAS records show that she experienced terrible anguish after this and tried to arrange to have them back multiple times. There was a brief time in the summer of 1967 when Clarence and Cheryl were returned to the care of Maureen — Clarence does not remember this. Unfortunately, after a month, Maureen once again gave up the children, unable to cope financially and emotionally according to CAS.

Although all the details of this time did not come to light until later in his life, as Clarence got to know Maureen as an adult and heard her brief explanation of why she agreed to place him in foster care, an old and deep misconception started to loosen its debilitating grip. Clarence had always believed that he had been abandoned because he was somehow not good enough:

 Now I know why. I've come to terms with why our mother gave us up, because she was really hoping that if she put us in the care of the CAS, hopefully by doing that she could give us a life better than the one that she could give us, or she could keep us away from being exposed to some of that stuff that could've possibly happened.

9

FAMILIES

In 1986, after spending a year in Toronto, living for roughly six months with each parent respectively, at twenty-one, Clarence decided to return to Kitchener.

> It was hard to live in Toronto. It was hard to make friends. It just seemed like everyone was so paranoid, and I wasn't very outgoing.

He found a spare room to live in with friends for a few months before finding his own apartment that he shared with a roommate. Soon enough, he had a chance encounter with an old friend downtown who told him that the Rumpel Felt Factory, located on the corner of Duke Street and Victoria Avenue, was hiring. Clarence applied for a job and was hired to work on a machine that blended bales of cotton or wool for rendering into felt. His job was to feed the bales into the machine and then transfer the blended materials to a conveyor that carried the raw material to other machines in the factory.

Clarence was a punctual and diligent employee. He got along well with his co-workers and worked hard. The problem was, whenever Clarence was working, his machine kept getting jammed. Before his first two weeks were up, his boss said he had two more weeks and then he was going to be let go. As far as Clarence was concerned, the issue wasn't totally his fault. Yes, he wasn't great at paying attention, but at the same time no one had properly trained him. He made a case to his employer: he wanted a second chance. So he was given two more weeks.

> One week went by, he [the boss] doesn't say nothing to me. He's just watching. Week and a half goes by, he doesn't say nothing. The last day comes of the two weeks. It's an hour or two until it's time to go. He comes up to me and he goes, 'Okay you have your job.'

Clarence proved himself during those two weeks, but he had also set a precedent. After that, his boss never missed a chance to grind his gears.

Clarence was so proud of his job at the factory that if he was up late partying he would come in a couple hours before the 7:30 a.m. shift and crash in the break-room — you can't miss a shift if you're already there. He spent a year working that position. Then his supervisor offered him a promotion: a lead-hand, in charge of six machines in the Finishing Department. Clarence took the job, and as soon as he did, his supervisor's attitude transformed. "He started teaching me things and looking at me as a valuable worker," says Clarence. With a full-time job and a place of his own, Clarence was feeling good. "I was walking down Victoria Street with a little bounce in my step," he says.

After working at the factory for a year and a half, Clarence left Rumpel Felt in 1988 for a new opportunity: the company that Stephanie's father worked for offered Clarence an apprenticeship job in the carpentry division of the organization. Around the same time, Clarence and Stephanie moved in together.

> We were dating for I don't know how many years by
> then. I think we talked about it and we thought it
> would be a good idea.

They rented a one-bedroom apartment in North Waterloo, near Conestoga Mall. Soon after, Clarence reconnected with the Reiers. He and Stephanie started visiting the Reiers, often during the holidays or for family gatherings.

It turned out that woodworking was not work that suited Clarence well. When a national recession hit in 1990, the company went into foreclosure and Clarence found himself unemployed. He did try his hand at house framing. "It was like minus twenty," he remembers, "and I was working with a crew and I said, 'Forget this.'" Then he heard from friends that a food distribution company was hiring and that the pay was not bad. Thinking about the fact that people always need food, no matter how tough it got, he applied and was able to secure a part-time position that involved assembling skids of groceries for distribution.

Lackie Brothers employee (1990)

Stephanie and Clarence had a mutual understanding that when Clarence attained full-time employment they would get married. But that plan changed in the fall of 1990 when Stephanie became pregnant. They decided to get married before she gave birth, and the wedding was set for February 1991. After borrowing some money, and with the help of gifts from family, Clarence and Stephanie married at a Catholic church in St Agatha, a small town just outside of Kitchener-Waterloo. The reception was held at New Dundee Community Centre. Both sets of Clarence's parents were at the wedding, his biological and foster parents. Many of his childhood friends were also there.

In the spring of 1991, Clarence and Stephanie were living in Kitchener, preparing for their first child. Clarence remembers quite vividly the day Stephanie went into labour:

> I was running around the apartment. I went and got the paternity book, and just flipping through stuff, just panicking. And then I assisted her into the car. We just got to the hospital when her water broke. And then I was like, 'Oh my goodness!' Right? 'Jesus, help me!' And we get into the room, and you can hear women screaming and crying — and my eyes are like the size of friggin' golf balls.
>
> But I was there with Steph, and I cried when Carleigh was born. It was such a beautiful thing. Tears came down out of my eyes, down my cheeks. It was hard to believe that I had a part in creating something so precious and beautiful.

Stephanie gave birth to Carleigh Cachagee in June 1991.

> With Carleigh, I think for the first years of Carleigh growing up she was with me all the time. Wherever I went, Carleigh went. We were like a team. And that was cool.

Over the next few years, life for Clarence consisted mostly of working, taking care of Carleigh, and visiting with family — which included the Reiers, the Cachagees, and Stephanie's family. Soon enough, Clarence was able to secure a full-time position at the grocer he worked for. He continued to party most weekends, which would usually include copious drinking and/or using weed. At some point that he doesn't recall exactly, he also started to experiment with cocaine.

> I can remember starting to do a bit more cocaine back then, but that was only at certain times, once or two times a year.

His substance use started to cause tension in his relationship with Stephanie.

> I think from almost the beginning, she knew that I struggled but she never really knew the depth of what I was living because I never even shared it with her, the traumas that I was living with and the things that had so much power over me.
>
> I put that woman through hell, but she kept giving me chances and kept giving me chances. It was a very co-dependent relationship. All I had to do was work. I'd hand my money over to her, and I'd always save some so that I could get weed or some booze. But she would take care of all of the bills. She would do everything. And that went on for a very long time.

Four years after Carleigh was born, Clarence and Stephanie had a second daughter, Madison Cachagee, born in October 1995.

> Madison Cree the Bumblebee. Madison was the cutest little kid. The same thing happened when she was born. Once again, I was overwhelmed that I was

part of making something so precious and beautiful. I was in the delivery room and I cried.

As new life came into the family, older life prepared to move on. A year after Madison was born, during Christmas holidays in 1996, Clarence's biological mother passed away. Maureen had epilepsy, and on the day she passed she had neglected to take her medication. It was during a visit to the family home near North Bay. She had a seizure while sleeping and by the time her family found her it was too late.

 That was a hard time in my life — finally getting to meet our mother. It was hard but reflecting on it, I was fortunate enough to spend sixteen years with her. It helped me understand the 'whys'. I can remember after she passed for a few years Steph and I would drive back to Toronto to visit my stepdad and my half-sister. It was hard leaving Toronto after every visit. I would always cry in the car due to the fact that a part of me was gone, like a wound was opened up. It was hard because it was like there was something missing for such a long time, and then that void was filled. When my mom passed that void was opened up again. Cheryl really took it hard.

I can remember that when my mom left us, making her journey to the spirit world, I started reading the Bible. I don't know if I was reading it to comfort me or to find something in there that would help me deal with the loss. I just remember I started reading the Bible.

Abby Cachagee (1991)

*When my mother died in '79 we were in this funeral chapel
up in Chapleau. And I walked out of the door, and she was
still inside.*

*And around the chapel there were hundreds and hundreds
of crows. They were on top of the roof. They were on the
wires. They were in the trees. And I knew then that all my
relations were there, both past and present. And it made me
happy.*

*Beside the door there were two coloured birds that had died.
I had never seen [them before]. I was still very angry so
rather than pick them up and bury them in a proper
manner, I just threw them in the bush.*

Clarence and Stephanie decided to save up for their first home. In 1999, they purchased a bungalow on Weber Street in Kitchener.

> Steph was a good mom. She was one hell of a woman. She took the responsibilities of a mother very seriously. She always looked after Carleigh and Madison. Even when they were small, Steph got up every night when they were crying. I did my best to be a father, but it was always drugs and alcohol in the background of my thinking, my motives. How could I do this and how could I get my needs met? It just blows me away how powerful, how cunning, baffling and powerful addiction can be. And reflecting back on when we first met and first started dating to when we bought our house, our relationship changed. We changed as people. We changed as a couple.

> I can remember when we bought the house, people said that the first year is the hardest. Well, every year we had that house it was hard.

That same year Clarence got a worrying phone call:

> I was working at Loblaws, and I got a call from my stepmom saying my dad was in the hospital. He had an accident. Steph and I got there, and it was a serious accident. He was in a coma.

Abby had fallen down a set of stairs. At the hospital the neurosurgeon asked to speak with Clarence. "If and when your father ever comes out of this coma, he will not be the same man that you knew him as," the doctor said, explaining that Abby had serious brain damage.

After consulting with his family, Clarence made one of the

most difficult decisions in his life. He decided to take Abby off life support.

> When he exhaled his last breath, I inhaled it, and he was gone. I think we had a Pipe Carrier come in while he was there, and some other traditional people came in to help him along his way to the spirit world. They put him on a train up to Chapleau.

It was Abby's brothers and sister who arranged to have the Pipe Carrier visit the hospital and organized the funeral at Fox Lake Reserve, Chapleau Cree First Nation.

> It's our customs and teachings that when someone passes away, we have a fire burning for four days. That's to honour the individual and it's also because it takes four days for that spirit to transition to the spirit world. During those four days the body is never left unattended. People come to the fire to say prayers and ask the Ancestors to come and find him and help him make that transition to the next world.

It was very cold and snowy at Fox Lake Reserve when the community held a celebration of life for Abby. A lot of people came out to pay their respects. Clarence was overwhelmed by it all.

> I probably wanted to run but I also wanted to be there to honour my dad and say something on behalf of the community. From what I can remember I said, 'This is all new to me, this culture, but I know that my dad would be really honoured to see all these people here who came to respect his passing.'

Abby Cachagee (1991)

And when I wear my Feathers, we are very symbolic. If I wear it up or if I wear it down. The manner in which I carry my Eagle Feathers tells another person how I feel, how much respect I give, how much honour there is in it. And there's nothing secretive about the ceremonies. They have been a practice. They relate to a circle. They relate to the directions. They relate to the grandfathers. And there's a peace. There's a peace. Finally I have a peace in me, an understanding. I can laugh again. I can talk. I'm not afraid anymore. And I'm not afraid of dying.

After Abby's passing, life back at home slowly started to unravel. Clarence recalls:

> Stephanie was working. I was working. I'd get frustrated. I never hit her, but we would argue a lot; we would bicker a lot. Then I'd get stressed out. She'd get stressed out. I'd usually go and drink or get high.

They decided to go to family counselling. Clarence showed up to the sessions with Stephanie, while Carleigh played with toys in the waiting area.

> But I did it for the wrong reason. My motive wasn't to address my faults or look at myself. It was just to satisfy her.

The stress of homeownership combined with Clarence's more frequent partying and use of drugs started to make family life dysfunctional. Stephanie told Clarence he had to go see a counsellor for addictions. He reluctantly agreed. He now recalls one visit to a therapist:

> After I sat down and I told him my story to the best of my ability, he just looked at me and he said, 'You know what?' He says, 'It's not your fault.' He says, 'The way you acted and the things you've done, it's not your fault, why you did it.' I think he was basically saying I was a product of my environment, what happened to me growing up.

What that therapist said about the importance of his story made an impression on Clarence, but he wasn't ready to confront his past. He recalls living a contradiction: sitting in one therapy session while thinking about some drugs that he had in his pocket.

After therapy, together with Stephanie or one-on-one, the relationship might improve for a little while, but it was only temporary — the real inner work had not begun.

> It'd go good for a while but then I'd always slip back into my old patterns because I didn't want to change. I didn't want to sober up. I didn't think I could function without drugs or alcohol.

At some point in 2001, Clarence started using cocaine more than cannabis. As his substance use increased, he started acting in more embarrassing ways around friends and family. He was losing control. That winter, Stephanie had had enough. Clarence recalls:

> I can't believe what I put her through. And I'm sorry for that. It wasn't my intention to do what I did to her and the girls. It's just that at that time in my life I had given up on being a husband. I had given up on being a father. I had given up on my responsibilities. I had given up on myself. And that's when she had enough. She gave me an ultimatum. She said you either pick the girls and me or drugs and alcohol. I remember having that conversation: I'm trying to process things; I'm trying to think, can I live without drugs and alcohol? And I'm saying, No, I can't. Because I didn't have any tools. I didn't have any confidence. I didn't have purpose. I didn't have meaning. I didn't have direction... We got in a big domestic. This was right after the ultimatum. And I can still see Steph standing in the basement, Carleigh and Madison crying, and me walking away. And when I did that, I walked away from myself.

When I pray today and when I think of all the people who have helped me in my life, who have been there, who have walked with me, who have held me, who have encouraged me, who have supported me, she's one of those people. And I thank her for it. And when I sing the Strong Woman Song, she's one of the women that I sing it for.

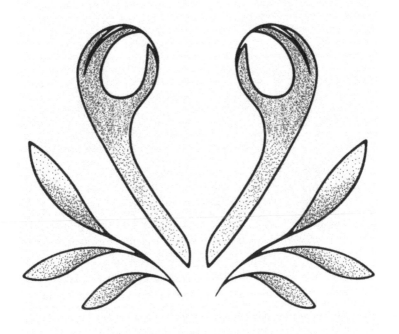

10

ABBY'S EARLY YEARS

The next object in the community bundle that I carry is a Warrior Club. The first club that was gifted to me, I received it from my uncle Michael. I've always wanted to carry a club because to me the club doesn't represent violence at all. It represents the values of a warrior that we all have inside of us. I believe a warrior is someone who advocates for those that don't have a voice. A warrior is one who watches over the water, watches over Mother Earth, advocates on behalf of the four-legged, and protects the Elders and the children. A warrior is someone who lives by the original teachings of the seven grandfathers and has a good heart and a good mind. I also believe a warrior is someone who puts the needs of others before themself.

I n 1943, Clarence's father, Clarence Hubert Cachagee, known as Abby, was born in Chapleau to Margaret Saylors and Howard Cachagee. Clarence is not aware when his father started going by the name Abby, but apparently the origin of that name comes from his resemblance to Li'l Abner from Al Capp's famous comic strip. Abby's father was enlisted in the army at the time of his birth and deployed overseas in the Second World War. When Howard returned two years later, he was unable or unwilling to provide for the family. A single mother and Survivor of the residential school system, Margaret struggled to take care of her children and in February of 1946 Abby was taken in by CAS and placed for adoption. Soon he was placed into the care of a French-Canadian family who were related by marriage to his mother. Reports on the conditions with this family were not good, as Abby explained:[1]

> *I was raised with dogs, my brother later told me. He says, 'you were tied up with the dogs about eight, nine hours a day.' And then they were my baby-sitters. So, for about a year and a half I spent my time with dogs.*[2]

Abby was taken back into the care of CAS and placed in a government shelter, which he recalls with mixed feelings:

> *I had good experiences in the shelter that I can remember. I was taken on a trip to Florida, later years I found out that had happened. And the majority of the time I spent at the shelter, there were times when I thought that I was the only person alone in my life, that I was an orphan. I had never known any family contact.*

At the age of five, Abby was brought to Moosonee to be placed in a residential school located on Moose Factory Island called Bishop Horden Hall. Abby recalled:

And getting to Moose Factory, one of my first things was
going around the little village and trying to crawl back in a
doghouse with a dog, and I got bit the first time. I didn't
learn my lesson then, so a few days later I went back again
and tried to crawl into the doghouse again ... and I got bit a
few times and they thought I would get an infection [rabies].
I had to go for these big needles and everything else.

On a barge crossing Moose River to Moose Factory Island,
Abby learned for the first time that he had siblings. A year before
he arrived, three of his brothers had also been sent to Moose
Factory, transferred there from St John's School after its closure in
1948. Abby only spoke French when he met them. Abby's brother
Michael Cachagee remembers a strained relationship among the
siblings, explaining, "If you've never had that opportunity of developing that sibling foundation, or that sibling connection, you know
they're your brothers and sisters, but at that age, until you develop
it later on in life, they're like strangers, you know, [in] some sense."[3]

When students arrived at Horden Hall they were assigned an
identification number and given a new English name, if they didn't
already have one. Their belongings were taken away and their hair
cut, procedures designed to erase evidence of Indigenous identity.
Physical conditions at the school were not good. Abby recalled that
the school building, which had no insulation, was notoriously cold
in the winter. Students would be set to work cutting, splitting, and
collecting firewood. Abby once witnessed horses fall through the
ice while pulling sleds loaded with chopped wood — the children
had to act quickly and cut loose the harnesses to save the sleigh.

The students weren't allowed to speak their Indigenous
languages; however, they found ways to resist, as Abby recalled:

We used to sit under our blankets at night. There would be
three or four of us; we'd put the blankets over our head and
we sit in a circle and we would start talking Cree.
They would tell stories in Cree, dreams. More so they talked

*in dreams. And that's — the dreams were old information of
things that their mothers and grandfathers and great grandfathers had talked about.*

Food at the school was bland and not very nutritious. Sometimes in the winter supplies would run low, so the children
resorted to catching birds and squirrels with slingshots. Abby even
recalled once being so hungry that he ate raw robin flesh. Michael
remembers a vivid conversation with a fellow student in which he
told him that he saw the staff washing maggots off the meat being
used for dinner.

Abby's positive memories during his time at Horden Hall were
about being allowed to leave the school grounds. He remembers
with warmth his time spent in the bush, exploring and trapping.
Holidays were always a welcome reprieve from the regimented
routine of the school. Sometimes, during the hunting seasons, Cree
hunters would set up "duck camps" across the river. On a couple of
occasions, Abby visited the people in their tents and was given tea
and bannock. He even once got to try beavertail: "It was ... it felt
like being home," he recalled. Throughout his time at the school,
Abby displayed a knack for languages. He was quick to learn to
speak Cree and English, and he was soon able to write them. By
the time he was ten, he began to act as an interpreter to help the
staff communicate with new students who did not speak English.

Abby's grandfather came to visit his children every year while
they were at Horden Hall. The first time he came, Abby recalls
that he and his brothers thought that he had come to take them
home. They were devastated when he left without them. In fact,
their grandfather was not allowed to bring them home; that was
prohibited by law. All he could do was come and see them each
year, and even then, he was not allowed to meet with them inside
the school grounds. They greeted each other through the chain link
fence.

In 1952 or '53, Abby's two older brothers were transferred to a
different residential school in Sault Ste Marie called Shingwauk

Hall. Abby, who was ten, stayed for a year in Moose Factory with his younger brother. Well-known to the staff as the school's interpreter, Abby managed to gain some privileges that year. He was sometimes allowed to eat with the adults. Their food was always much better than what was served to the children. "They had meat; they had vegetables; they had potatoes, fresh potatoes," he said.

The next year Abby was transferred to Shingwauk Hall where he was reunited with his older brothers. His younger brother was left on his own at Horden Hall for another year.

By the time that Abby arrived at Shingwauk Hall in 1954, the school had long ago drifted away from its founding principles derived from its namesake, the Anishinaabe chief, Shingwaukonse.

THE STORY of Shingwauk's vision for education begins in the early nineteenth century with Chief Shingwauk and his Anishinaabe community of the Upper Great Lakes. Shingwauk was a leader with many gifts. After fighting alongside the British in the War of 1812, he became a chief for his Nation.

Faced with rapid European settlement and encroachment, Chief Shingwauk endeavoured to find a way for his people to thrive in a changing landscape. In the early 1800s, the Nation he belonged to relocated to Garden River, hoping to build a community modelled after European agriculture practices and supported by income from the sale of natural resources.[4] Shingwauk believed that in order to survive the colonization of white settlers, his community would need a European education. He also thought that it was important to learn Christianity because to him the Christian God seemed to provide settlers with strength and power.[5]

After seeking guidance from the spirit world through fasting, he was granted a vision in which he saw an English missionary come to his people to teach them.[6] He held a counsel with his community and then led a delegation to York (now Toronto) to meet with the British governor who agreed to send a missionary and provide funding to build European-style buildings on the reserve. Rev William McMurray, an Anglican missionary, was assigned to the task. In 1833, the reverend assisted Shingwauk's community in the construction of several buildings, including a small schoolhouse located in what is now the city of Sault Ste Marie.[7]

Over the next few decades Shingwauk's descendants carried forth the vision of a self-sufficient First Nation guided by traditional wisdom with the addition of European skills and religion.[8] Over time, though, it became clear that this vision of cross-cultural equality was not shared by the British (and, later, Canadians) who worked with them. For colonial bureaucrats and Christian missionaries, their goal was to change the Anishinaabe people by erasing their Indigenous culture and making them as indistinguishable from Euro-Christian society as possible.

An important change to the way the school was run occurred in 1871 when the Anglican church suspended missionary work in Garden River. Augustine (Ogista) Shingwauk, son of Chief Shingwauk, was upset to lose someone who had become a valuable ally in political negotiations with the colonial government. He traveled to Toronto without consulting his community to ask an Anglican committee to reconsider their decision. Shingwauk requested a new missionary and financial support for building a large "teaching wigwam" where Indigenous children could learn skills needed for the modern economy.[9] On his way home, he managed to raise some funds through speaking engagements in St Catharines and Hamilton.

Shingwauk was able to convince the Anglican committee to continue their mission, and they dispatched Rev Edward Wilson to Garden River. Soon after Wilson arrived, he and some of the Garden River community agreed that the small schoolhouse should be expanded. They raised funds in England and began construction on a new, bigger school. The idea was to construct a large building in the same manner of other industrial schools that were being operated by missionaries across the country. The building was completed in 1873, but six days later, the school burnt down in a mysterious fire that was rumoured to have been set by community members who were opposed to the project.[10]

After the fire, more funds were raised; however, this time the school was built in a new location at a distance from the Garden River reserve. In 1875, the new three-storey Shingwauk Home opened on the north shore of St Marys River. Notably, as the school distanced itself physically from the Garden River First Nation, it also did so ideologically. For Shingwauk the school was meant to preserve the Anishinaabe community as a distinct people, while Wilson was more focused on assimilating the students into Canadian culture.[11] Early in its operation, Wilson expressed pride over the fact that "not a word of Indian is heard from our boys after six months." Wilson was proud to participate in and witness cultural genocide. Lack of enrolment from local Anishinaabe communities made it clear that they no longer supported the educational goals of the school. Indeed, the spirit of cooperation and equality that had guided earlier collaboration among the Garden River Anishinaabe and European missionaries had almost completely disappeared.[12]

The Shingwauk school operated according to a strict routine. Students were awakened at 6:00. The boys did chores like milking cows and cleaning the stables, and the girls prepared breakfast, which was served at 7:00. Morning prayer began at 7:30. Thirty minutes later, the students were split into two groups, one would work during the morning and one would take classes. After some free time to play, classes and work for the two groups began at 8:45 and ended at 11:45 so students could break for lunch. Then the groups alternated for the afternoon until 4:00 when they were allowed free time until dinner at 5:30. After dinner, upper year students were set to studying and lower year students were put to work on chores. After evening prayers, the students were put to bed. Student labour was supposedly for educational purposes, but in many ways, it was needed to keep the institution afloat with upkeep and enterprise.

Although Wilson was an early advocate of the residential school's project of forced assimilation, after several years of running the school, he grew disillusioned. In 1891, he published an anonymous article expressing concern that the school was doing more harm than good.[13] In 1893, Wilson resigned from his position as principal. The church authorities who undertook operation of the school were even more removed from a relationship with the Anishinaabe. Over the next several years, the Shingwauk Home followed a more aggressive policy of assimilation. The school was chronically underfunded and nearly closed in 1910. By 1935, the Anglican diocese negotiated with the federal government to formally become part of Canada's residential school system.

When Abby arrived at Shingwauk Hall, he was surprised to discover another family member he hadn't known about:

> *But coming down to Shingwauk in 1954 was the first time I met my sister. I never knew I had a sister either. And I met my sister here. And my brothers were already here, and I showed up. And finally, a year later, my youngest brother showed up. So, we were all together as a family unit.*

Like their brother Michael, Abby's sister Marjorie says that it was difficult for the siblings to hug each other and feel comfortable around one another.[14] Even though their sister was also at the school, Abby and his brothers rarely had the chance to see her because teachers and administrators made sure to segregate genders in the institution. "The only time I could talk to my sister," said Abby, "was at night after meals. I used to have to sneak around the building, going to talk to her through the screen over on the girl's side."

During the time that Abby lived there, Shingwauk Hall provided boarding for Indigenous children while they attended a public school nearby during the day. Life at the school was very regimented. Students were marched to school in the morning and marched home in the afternoon, at which point they were put to work on maintenance at the institution. And the harsh conditions they had experienced at Holden Hall persisted at Shingwauk: the food was lousy and the building was frigid during the winter. When visitors came, they were only allowed to see the students for fifteen minutes — despite having sometimes made a journey of hundreds of kilometres.

Until he had a growth spurt, Abby often experienced physical abuse from older boys at the school. Loneliness and hunger hardened the children and intensified ethnic divisions. The issue was made worse by a lack of supervision. In addition to violence, Abby witnessed staff sexually abuse students at Shingwauk. His recollection echoes the stories of thousands of other Survivors:

> We used to, the older boys and myself, we would try to do as much to stop it. So, what we used to do is we would take our belts and tie them across the beds at night, and we'd make an obstacle course for the supervisor, who'd come in and he would try to feel up the younger boys under the blanket and so forth.
> We would hear him coming and then all of the sudden we'd hear him falling — boom! boom! — moaning and groaning... And then... the boots would start flying. In the morning you could see his face would be swollen up and his lip would be cut.

Being located close to the city of Sault Ste Marie, students had different kinds of opportunities off the school grounds than they had at Moose Factory. Older students would sometimes go into town and try to find odd jobs. But Abby recalled that it was unwise to gather in a group, since doing so would attract racism from the townsfolk. Abby remembered having the chance to go to the movies. Often students would pool their money and buy treats from the general store nearby, purchasing maybe a box of crackers and jam, or a loaf of bread.

Abby's sister Marjorie says that he grew into a handsome young man. At some point, a teacher even painted a portrait of him. In 1958, when he was fifteen years old, Abby graduated from Shingwauk.

His brother Michael sums up the residential schooling experience in a light-hearted way: "It was like walking through a carwash and trying to stay dry." But in an interview quoted in Volume 4 of the Final Report of the TRC in Canada on 'Missing Children and Unmarked Burials', Michael also disclosed the gruesome horrors that he witnessed: "Students had to help dig the graves... [and] because the graves dug in the winter were shallow, in the spring, bears would root about in the cemetery and feed on the student remains."[15]

Despite having finally escaped the repressed life of residential school, Abby left with very few skills and tools for living. He then experienced what so many other Survivors felt after leaving residential schools: he was caught between two worlds — traditional Cree society and the dominant white, Euro-Christian society.

PERHAPS SEEKING MEANING, purpose, and direction of his own, soon after graduating, Abby made his way to the city of North Bay and enlisted in the Canadian military, as his father and grandfather had before him. It was in North Bay that he met Maureen Lindsay, a young woman of Scottish and Irish descent. They were young lovers — Abby nineteen years old and Maureen fifteen — and planned to get married at an Anglican church in March of 1963. However, on the day of the wedding, Abby did not make an appearance. He had had a wild night before the wedding, getting into a competition with his friends to see who could steal the most cars in one evening. Abby won the contest; he also ended up in jail, effectively leaving Maureen at the altar. Nonetheless, sometime later, Maureen and Abby were officially married.

Those early years of marriage were somewhat tumultuous; Abby and Maureen moved to Kitchener, trying to make ends meet in a city with more job opportunities and some family connections. In autumn, Abby was once again arrested for car theft. Expecting a baby, Maureen returned to the North Bay area to live with her grandparents. Over the next couple of years, Abby tried to support the family but he struggled with alcohol use, which often accompanied his involvement with crime, and he had mental health challenges — both likely stemming from his involvement in the residential school system. When Clarence was born in 1965, that same month Abby's father passed away due to health issues from excessive drinking.

Clarence recalls a story that Abby shared with him once, which Clarence suspects is from this time in Abby's life. Abby said that he had once lost the will to live; full of despair, he sat down in the middle of a highway, intending to be run over by a passing vehicle. It was likely this moment that is described in CAS records as an episode of severe depression which involved the police in August of 1966. Abby was admitted into a hospital after his mental health crisis and Maureen's situation with the children quickly deteriorated thereafter, leading to that fateful fall.

In November, Abby was again present in Kitchener but he was once again incarcerated on November 3 and the children were taken in by CAS the day after. From jail in Waterloo, Abby was transferred to a hospital out of town for psychiatric care. He wrote to CAS during this time, expressing interest in his children and asking for information about how he could take care of them. On March 9, 1967, Abby was released from the hospital and visited the CAS office in Kitchener. He told the social worker there that he planned to find employment and hoped to take care of the children. Unfortunately, in April, he was charged again with car theft and he left town on bail. His relationship with Maureen had soured by this point, although they were still legally married.

Abby was incarcerated again in January of 1968, presumably when police identified him in Toronto. He was sentenced to one year in prison. During this time, he wrote regularly to CAS inquiring about his children. Abby tried to clarify how Indian Affairs were involved and he ensured that the children would retain their Indian Status if they were adopted. He was also anxious to know if the children would be put up for adoption without his consent. CAS informed Abby that the children would retain their status in the event of adoption, and that he would be required to make the decision for adoption — although the records do not indicate how this was accomplished while Abby was in prison. He was informed in February that the children were made Crown Wards and that CAS was seeking an adoptive placement for them.

Many years later, Clarence learned how his own story had uncanny similarities to that of his father: from their early involvement with the child welfare system, their excessive drinking at a young age, to how they both formed young relationships with their future wives. Like his father, Clarence was neither able to nurture a healthy and lasting relationship with his wife Stephanie, nor could he remain a present and supportive parent for their two young children.

11

THE CYCLE

After Stephanie and Clarence separated in 2001, Clarence moved out of the home they had purchased in Waterloo. Those first few days on his own were rough ones.

> I remember I was driving somewhere, and I was so depressed that I thought it would be easy to just take my car and drive it into the other lane, into oncoming traffic.

Thankfully, he didn't act on the impulse — he can say now that that was the only time he ever had any kind of suicidal ideation.

He moved in with a friend who rented him a room, and Clarence started making a plan for moving forward. After a few months, the house on Weber Street was sold, and Clarence was served papers to appear in family court. They arranged a visiting schedule for their two daughters. In the midst of this life upheaval, he started drinking and using substances more often.

About a year after the divorce, the grocery company that had employed Clarence for twelve years relocated its warehouse and restructured the organization. When the company began evaluating employees, Clarence's assessment was mediocre, at best. Some of his co-workers warned him that when he was transferred to the new warehouse, he was going to face increased scrutiny under new management. It was no surprise, then, when the company offered a severance package: twenty-one thousand dollars. Thinking about his poor impression on new management, as well as his current life circumstances, he took the package and left employment. This was in the spring of 2002.

"I knew with half a year's salary and my addiction," Clarence says, "if I didn't do something, I'd end up dead." After receiving the money Clarence decided to quit drinking.

> I wanted to prove to myself that I had enough willpower, that if I put my mind to it, I could quit doing everything.

Then he paid some child support in advance, bought his two daughters a season's pass to the local waterpark, and purchased a new car.

Clarence started spending time with his stepbrother, who was on his own healing journey and had been sober for several years. Over the next few months, Clarence sporadically worked for him in Toronto. For the most part, though, Clarence was unemployed while he lived off his severance. Perhaps due to some persuasion from his stepbrother (and maybe even his ex-wife), Clarence was convinced that it might be a good idea to start attending an Alcoholics Anonymous group. His stepbrother told him about a meeting on Park Street in an old factory building. After some deliberation Clarence decided to go. He recalls the experience of showing up to his first meeting:

> I saw all these people standing around outside, some of them were laughing; they were smoking. And I was scared. I wanted to run. But I also wanted to prove to myself that, hey, you can do this on your

own and let's just go and see what this is all about, the fellowship of AA.

Clarence opened the door and walked up the staircase and entered a large room. On a small table off to the side, beside a plate of cookies, there was a percolating coffee pot. Rays of hot sunshine were streaming in through the windows, lighting some AA slogans posted on the walls.

This too shall pass.
One day at a time.
But for the grace of God.

The chairs were arranged in a circle in the middle of the room. There were fifteen or so people mingling, getting ready for the meeting to start.

> I saw a door on the other side of the room, and I could see other people sitting in there, so I kept walking. I could see another door leading into a third room, so I kept walking. In the third room there wasn't another door; I could not escape.

Out of exit options, he finally sat down. It turned out that the third room, which Clarence unintentionally found, was for newcomers.

> That's where I learned about the first three steps of AA. In the first step, we admitted that we were powerless over alcohol — that our lives had become unmanageable. Everybody would go around the circle and talk about that. We would share our own experience of being powerless over alcohol. And then we would share how that experience had led to our lives being unmanageable.

Then we talked about the second step, which is coming to believe that a power greater than ourselves can restore us to sanity. This is where we had to come to an understanding of where our thinking gets us; and then we had to learn how to ask for help from a power that's greater than us.

Number three is making a decision to turn our will and our lives over to the care of God as we understood him. In that meeting we talked about the first three steps.

The man who chaired the meeting was a straight shooter. After introductions and sharing around the circle, he was the first to start probing Clarence with questions.

> I said I was just there to check it out, see what AA's all about. And he says, 'Well, don't you think you have a problem?' I said, 'Well, I'm not drinking, and I did it all on my own.' He says, 'That's bullshit. This is where you need to be. You know what? You're only fooling yourself.'

Clarence felt his face go red. He remained silent and resolved on the spot to stay only until the end of the meeting. "I vowed to never go back to an AA meeting again," he says.

Now Clarence admits that the man was right. It was a comical self-deception to claim that he didn't have a problem. Still, the moderator could have probably been a bit more gentle.

> It's places like that where you get called out on stuff. They're there to make you see things for the first time. I was shameful, scared, pissed off that he called me out. But he was right; he was totally right. I thought that he had audacity to call me out in front of

people. It made me feel like I was getting scolded and that I was in trouble.

Clarence didn't go back to AA for a very long time.

Two months after he had quit alcohol, Clarence started using drugs more frequently, especially cocaine. This expensive habit continued for the next few months, until his severance money was spent — it had only been about six months since leaving his job. He went looking for work again and soon found employment at a water packaging facility in Aberfoyle, a thirty-minute commute from Kitchener. The job had a continental work schedule which meant that Clarence worked a rotation of day, evening, and night shifts. "It was a fast-paced environment," he says, explaining that he often used stimulants to stay awake during the night shifts.

After the divorce, Clarence still made time to see his daughters, trying to stay connected. He would sometimes take them on outings, to the local waterpark for instance, or they might go visit relatives.

> I tried for about the first two years after my marriage fell apart. I tried to be responsible as a father, but I wasn't very responsible.

He remembers one time while they were at a waterpark, that he ran out to his car to use drugs.

> At that time in my life. What kind of father was I, you know? It just makes me sick. To know that drugs were more important to me than the safety and well-being of my two important children. But that seemed normal, that seemed to be what I lived for.

By the summer of 2003, while working at the water packaging plant, Clarence had been abstaining from alcohol for about sixteen months. But he was white-knuckling it. He had no supports. He had no plan. And he was doing it for others, to prove to his friends and family that he didn't have a problem. But when an intimate relationship fell apart, Clarence started drinking again.

His drug use followed suit and was soon spiralling out of control. After a year of working in Aberfoyle, he simply stopped showing up. Soon after leaving work, Clarence's drivers license was suspended because he hadn't kept up with child support payments. He started to experience a more transient lifestyle, sleeping wherever he could.

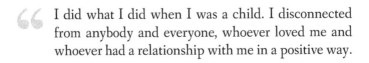

> I did what I did when I was a child. I disconnected from anybody and everyone, whoever loved me and whoever had a relationship with me in a positive way.

Leaving his job at the water packaging facility began a cycle in Clarence's life that would last for the next several years. It went something like this: Clarence would work for twelve to eighteen months, holding it together as a functioning addict; then, after catching up on child support, he would leave his job and spend the next several months partying and surviving, living in various places, on a friend's couch, at a shelter, or on the street in a state of transient homelessness; after he had enough, or after he fell too far behind on child support, he would find work and start the cycle all over again.

In 2004, after a few months of unemployment and transient homelessness, Clarence managed to get a job as a lead hand of receiving at a distribution warehouse, supervising inbound and outbound shipments. Sometimes he was in charge of a team of fifty employees. Often, while on the job, Clarence would be, as he puts it, "all buggered up." Usually high on cocaine, he would purposely keep the shift introductions short and quick so he could go off and spend the day alone. He started behaving more erratically at work, calling in sick because he was partying too much, or getting into arguments with his co-workers — he was even suspended once for threatening another employee.

Despite his unstable living arrangements, Clarence still made time to see his daughters and visit relatives. Clarence recalls purchasing them gifts, hoping to make an impression. Yet the signs of his lifestyle did not go unnoticed by Carleigh and Madison. He remembers one time, while out for a drive with them, that Madison noticed his thumb and asked if he had hurt himself. He hid his hand in shame because it was burned and calloused from smoking crack, even though he had not been using it very often at that point.

Sometimes his lifestyle would have a more drastic impact on his daughters' lives. He remembers a day when his ex-wife asked him to pick up the girls from dance practice one evening. He agreed, but when the time came, he never showed up because he was distracted by drugs.

> It's stuff like that. It just eats at me today... I was the perfect definition of a deadbeat dad. But I'm so glad that Stephanie was there as a mother for our daughters because I wasn't there. I wasn't capable.

Eventually his daughter Carleigh had enough of being let down by her dad and said she didn't want to see him anymore. Clarence started seeing his daughters less and less, detaching by degrees every year.

> I was consumed with so much shame that I didn't want to see them because I thought it would be better if I was out of their life as their father in the condition that I was in. I did the one thing I said I would never do. I abandoned my own daughters. I said I would never do that because I knew how it feels and how painful it is. It's actually very sad how that intergenerational trauma can flow right into the next generation.

He descended deeper into a life of addiction, embracing the numbing band-aid of substance use.

> When I got caught in the grips of addiction even more, it's like I just disconnected from everything. I disconnected from my daughters. I disconnected from my sister. I disconnected from my family. I disconnected from everything and anybody that loved me. And then I even disconnected from myself because that's what drugs and alcohol do: you use them to escape. And then I just escaped.

Clarence guesses that there was a stretch of two to five years where he never saw his children.

Becoming less and less dependable due to his substance use, Clarence left his job at the shipping warehouse and entered a second episode of heavy substance use. As Clarence's life was consumed by drugs, he started eating less and sleeping less. He was at the same time forming unhealthy intimate relationships, associating more with people who also struggled with addictions.

> Right around that time I was going out with female crack dealers. I was running drugs for them. I was exchanging drugs for sex. And I — it took me awhile to accept — I always said that I was a crack user; I didn't want to accept that I was a "crackhead" because once you were a crackhead you were stereotyped, you were put into a different category.
>
> It was dirty; it was grimy. It brought me shame. And I can remember one time... looking in the mirror, and my face was sunken in. I was eating like once every two or three days. I was up for days. I didn't even want to look at myself in the mirror. It was disgusting; it was hideous. It felt like I was going to self-destruct. I totally disconnected from everything.

And it was so astounding, how such a little piece of something, which could be the size of your baby fingernail or half that size, could have so much power over you.

By the summer of 2006, Clarence's drug use was obvious to everyone around him — though, he still insisted that he didn't have a problem. Unconvinced, that summer some of his friends set up a scenario to force Clarence to acknowledge he had a problem — an odd sort of approach to an "intervention," which was bound to fail.

One of Clarence's friends owned a farm in Wellesley township, about half an hour's drive from Kitchener. One day, this friend picked up Clarence along with and another mutual friend Jacob,[1] who was also struggling with substance use, and drove them out to the farm. It wasn't until after they got to the farm that he showed Clarence and Jacob how they would be keeping themselves occupied for the next few weeks: they were tasked with cleaning and packaging the harvest of a cannabis grow-op hidden among the farm's crops.

> He just brought us cases of beer. We cleaned his weed for him, and we ate when we wanted to and slept. One day was okay. Second day wasn't too bad. And then it's like the third day, Jacob and I were just going: 'This is fucked. We gotta get out of here.'

Needless to say, the approach failed to force Clarence to admit he had a problem. Clarence and Jacob wandered the country roads until they found people at another farm who were willing to drive them and hitched a ride back to Kitchener, back to the city.

Clarence's life in the city was mostly characterized by socializing, drinking, and using drugs.

> I would always have aspirations or thoughts of changing things, of maybe looking for a job, maybe

doing a resume, maybe calling my sister. But along the way somehow it would always get derailed.

He was sleeping wherever he could, usually on a friend's couch or at the men's shelter at House of Friendship. Money was always an issue, and sometimes he went to extreme lengths to make ends meet.

 I was doing some things to people that I'm not proud of today. I was extorting money.

It started one evening when someone tried stealing drugs from Clarence while hanging out with him and his friends. Clarence caught him in the act. He later visited the individual's workplace and told him to pay up or he'd start destroying his property.

In 2007, Clarence had a falling out with Geoff, a long-time friend.[2] Clarence thought of this man as an older brother and they had been roommates for a few months. The conflict started one day when Geoff accused Clarence of stealing money from him. Clarence denied it. He was offended that such a close friend would accuse him of stealing. Geoff told Clarence to get out of his house and get out of his life. "That really pissed me off," says Clarence.

A few weeks after he had been evicted, he was drinking with a friend. Puffed up on alcohol, he returned to Geoff's place hollering and yelling. The confrontation turned ugly when Geoff came out with a shovel in hand. He hit Clarence in the head and jabbed him in the stomach. Clarence grabbed Geoff's hair, shoved his thumb into his mouth, and pulled him to the ground. He picked up a brick nearby and raised it into the air, only to be stilled by a friend who was watching the fight: "Clare, fuckin' don't do it!" Clarence tossed the brick aside and left Geoff there on the ground. They never reconciled.

Two weeks later, when Clarence was under the influence, he saw the man he had extorted money from earlier that year and attacked him, intending to extort from him again. Bystanders called the police who arrested Clarence. At the same time, Clarence found out that Geoff had pressed charges for the assault. The two offences were serious enough that in October 22, 2007, Clarence was sentenced to five months in prison with an eighteen-month probation order. This time he was sent to Maplehurst Correctional Complex in Milton, Ontario.

12

SURVIVING

In January 2008, three months after being admitted, Clarence was released from the Maplehurst Correctional Complex. He was very relieved to be getting out. Staff handed over his possessions, which included a half-full bottle of sherry at the bottom of his backpack.

> Sitting at the bus stop in Milton, we were — there was like three or four other guys there — we were drinking the booze, and one guy had cigarettes. We were smoking tailor-mades and drinking some gut-rot sherry, living high on the hog.

So, it was back to the same old cycle of transient homelessness: work for several months, quit, party, and repeat.

> It was a big blur... It's like a day turned into a week and a week turned into a month. I had good intentions of doing things, or doing a resume, or going and finding a job. Sometimes I would, like every year and a half I'd find a job, pay off my child support.

After being released from prison, Clarence returned to Kitchener and started staying at House of Friendship's men's shelter again. He also started to frequent St John's Kitchen, a resource centre downtown that served a daily hot lunch. Jennifer Mains, who was the coordinator at the kitchen, recalls when Clarence first started to appear there.[1] He struck her as a man with a strong spirit, but in a tough walk of life. They got to know each other and soon became friends.

Clarence quickly started to feel a sense of belonging at the Kitchen. People there didn't judge him for who he was. He met some outreach workers and began to develop relationships with them. Clarence also met some peers who also struggled with alcohol use. They soon became good friends, often hanging out together near the train station.

> That was my family. Being an addict and especially being an alcoholic, if you didn't have any money, other alcoholics would help you out. There was a certain loyalty there; they knew how much you were hurting so they would give you a couple drinks.

In part due to his experience driving a forklift and a referral from a friend, Clarence was able to find work at a shipping pallet company. He worked there all summer while renting a room downtown. A typical day involved meeting up with friends in the morning at the train station, picking up some lunch to-go from St John's Kitchen, and then heading into work in the afternoon, "half-buzzed." After six months at the pallet company, Clarence switched positions to a cold storage facility, which was under the same ownership. In the midst of all this, he lost his rental unit, so he ended up homeless for a few months, sleeping in churches or at the shelter while continuing to work. Eventually he found a place to live on Laurel Street in Waterloo.

Regular use of cocaine is an expensive habit — and Clarence's budget was tight with fifty percent of his pay cheque automatically withheld for child support. It was coincidental, then, when one day his drug supplier's package of cocaine included crystallized rocks among the powder. Clarence asked about the rocks in the bag and his dealer said that, if he wants them, he could have them. Clarence knew exactly what they were: crack cocaine, the freebase form of cocaine, a crystallized variant of the stimulant that was smoked rather than snorted and provided a more powerful and shorter lasting high.

Clarence had used crack cocaine before on occasion but generally chose to avoid it because of the stigma that the drug had. Over the months he began to use it more frequently — "it was easier to find crack cocaine than it was to find powder back in those days," he explains. As his drug use increased, it began to take over his life.

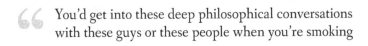

> Sometimes I would get so buzzed. I had my dealer's phone number on my work phone, but it was so close to one of the management's numbers that I called the management up once (or even twice I think) and I asked them if they could get me a couple grams. I said, 'Can you get me a forty-piece?' She said, 'Clarence is this you?' She says, 'You want me to bring you a 40-ouncer?!' Click! Thank goodness she thought it was a forty-ouncer of booze.

Daily life became quite chaotic. Clarence remembers staying up for days on end, watching the sun rise and set, again and again, only to sleep for a few hours and get started all over again. Missing one waking hour was missing a chance to get high. Often these lengthy episodes would end with psychotic hallucinations. "I was surprised how long you could go without your body needing any food," Clarence reflects. He also started to imagine a different kind of life:

> You'd get into these deep philosophical conversations with these guys or these people when you're smoking

crack and you'd be dreaming about what you want to do or what you could do. I said, 'You know what? I want to be a helper. I want to help people because I know what it's like to suffer. I know what trauma is about. I want to help people.'

At the same time, unhindered crack use was taking a toll on his body and mind. He could hardly face himself in the mirror; he could hardly even recognize his reflection.

> It just ripped my soul right apart. It's not like I wasn't depressed or bummed out or lost enough, but when you start doing that stuff it just takes you even deeper. It's like it opens a trapdoor and you fall right into the bowels of a cesspool of sorrow. You just drop right in there. And you just become consumed. Your every waking hour is trying to get some more of that stuff.

As Clarence's use of crack cocaine became too much for his body and his life, he decided he really needed to stop. His solution was to substitute crack for a different but familiar dependency — alcohol. As Clarence puts it, "I hit the booze really hard to get off that stuff." From then on, whenever the cravings started, Clarence would simply drink himself into oblivion. That winter of 2008-09, Clarence's substance use gave way to a deep alcoholism. In the morning, he would struggle to keep down his first drink, often mixing hard alcohol with water so that he could stomach it.

In the summer of 2009, Clarence was laid off at his job at the cold storage facility and began receiving unemployment insurance. He returned to a life in shelters, on couches, and sometimes on the street. Most days followed the same pattern. In the morning, Clarence would stroll the streets — sometimes he felt pretty good about his life, saying hello to folks, checking in with friends, being known around town, and understood. At noon, Clarence would meet up with the crew at their spot and pool their money. Someone would make the run to the liquor store and after having a few drinks, they'd make their way around town, maybe go visit a friend's place, following the whims of the group, seeking the next place to socialize and drink. Most of the time Clarence would follow the group around town, until he became so drunk that he could no longer keep up. "I'd just disappear," he says, describing one incident when he stumbled over to a corner at the bus terminal and stooped to the ground as his friends boarded the bus.

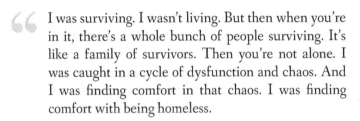

> I was surviving. I wasn't living. But then when you're in it, there's a whole bunch of people surviving. It's like a family of survivors. Then you're not alone. I was caught in a cycle of dysfunction and chaos. And I was finding comfort in that chaos. I was finding comfort with being homeless.

ON THE CORNER of Victoria Avenue and Weber Street in downtown Kitchener sits an unassuming two-storey industrial building. Made of the yellow brick ubiquitous in the area, it was a button factory in the bygone days of a booming textile industry. It was also not far from the streets that Clarence was living on in Kitchener-Waterloo. In 2006, the building was purchased and renovated by a non-profit organization called The Working Centre. On the main floor is a second-hand store called Worth a Second Look, and the second floor is the home of St John's Kitchen, a renovated community space that serves a hot lunch on weekdays and provides a place for people to socialize and connect with outreach workers.

St John's Kitchen originated in 1984, in the gymnasium of St John the Evangelist Anglican Church on Water Street, which is not far from its present location. The Working Centre started the initiative in collaboration with the church as a resource centre for people who were unemployed. Their funding ran out after a year but by then it had become a popular refuge for marginalized community members. Fortunately, with some help from House of Friendship, the Kitchen stayed open and began serving a meal every day.[2] Within a couple of years, staff and volunteers were serving 4,200 meals a month. As the Kitchen's popularity increased, it became clear that a new space was needed. After twenty-two years at St John's Church, the Kitchen relocated a few blocks away.

The new space was renovated to be open concept, with large windows and bright walls. It had a much homier atmosphere than the church gymnasium. The kitchen itself is totally visible from the main space, separated only by a countertop — anyone can see what the cooks are up to or chat with whoever is making a meal that day.

From early on, organizers of the Kitchen sought to break down barriers between staff, volunteers, and patrons, trying to nurture a spirit of hospitality that provided opportunities for anyone to get involved. They wanted to avoid becoming a so-called "staunchy social service." Moreover, coordinators believed that the participation of patrons would engender a feeling of ownership and belonging.

By 1999, homelessness had become more prevalent in Kitchener and patrons at the Kitchen had increasingly complex needs. Jennifer Mains helped incorporate more outreach services, such as a health clinic. She also continued to advocate for a kind of service that promoted equality between worker and community members, changing the dynamic of the relationship, as she explained: "We walk with people only. That is what we do. We are not setting goals. We are not case managers. I am not trying to improve that person's life. I am not out there to see if I can get that person to change." She insists, rather, "That is not the issue. The point is to ask, 'Where are you? What do you need help with?' And when the person says, 'You know, I think I want to go to detox,' to respond so that there is no pressure ... It is the person leading the way — we are supporting."[3]

The new clinic housed the Psychiatric Outreach Project. One of the family doctors in the project was George Berrigan. After he retired from his family practice in 2008, he wanted to continue working part-time with low-income clients. He ended up at St John's Kitchen treating individuals who struggled with homelessness or substance use, often both. Usually, these struggles are concurrent with mental health challenges. George readily admits that, before he got started, he had no training in the field of addictions, as was the case with most doctors in Canada at the time. He had to hit the books (and the internet).

One lesson he learned early on, which he emphasizes now, is that addiction issues are highly related to negative childhood experiences. Referring to Gabor Maté's book *In the Realm of Hungry Ghosts*, George explains: "Most people who have severe addiction issues have had horrific childhood experiences: neglect, losing their parents early in their life or never ever knowing who their parents were, going through different types of families as they were growing up, never really making any attachments, never getting any sense of who they were — that's disastrous."[4] When he got started at St John's Kitchen, George brought with him an ability to build relationships with clients, something that proved essential to the community he was working with. But, at the same time, he realized that the standard practices he had been trained in were not going to work with this community.

Jennifer believed these challenges required a different kind of response. George found insight in the harm reduction approach, explaining: "The concept in harm reduction is that it's more important to get the person who's addicted to survive than get him or her into abstinence right away. And so the reality of the harm reduction approach is primarily dealing with the problems as you have them as efficiently as you can, accepting the fact that you can't cure the addiction immediately and in some cases maybe never, but you can reduce the harm."

When Clarence reflects on St John's Kitchen, he has a lot to say about its impact on his own life and the people involved in the work there:

> Those people, George and Jennifer, were inspirational at that time in my life, because they didn't judge me. They had compassion. They offered me unconditional support and I knew it was genuine; it was from the heart because they cared and they always had my best interest in mind. It was love that I was starting to feel, unconditional love, which was a strange experience.
>
> They were showing me and teaching me how to have a good heart and a good mind, which ran parallel with me striving to become a helper. There were many, many more people who walked with me and helped me.

Since 2008, Clarence had been in a relationship with a woman who was also struggling with addictions.

> We were living on the streets. We were sleeping in churches. We rented two rooms together. We were both alcoholics; we were both addicts. It was a very, very, crazy, distorted relationship.

Realizing that they were both struggling, the two started reaching out for professional help. One such moment was in 2008 when Clarence and his partner visited a large house on College Street downtown Kitchener that housed The Healing of the Seven Generations, an Indigenous resource centre addressing the legacy of Canada's residential school system.

It was obvious they were both in rough shape when they entered, yet Clarence did not feel judged. A soothing aroma from burnt sage lingered in the air. There was a big bulletin board near the door filled with posters for events, resources for treatment, slogans and inspiring poems. They found a few people mingling about in the common rooms at a long table and in an adjacent room where chairs were arranged in a circle. Eventually, someone led Clarence and his partner upstairs to speak with a woman named Donna Dubie, who is Haudenosaunee from Six Nations. She remembers when they first came into her office: "He wore his hurt," she says. "His face was smashed up, black and blue. He came in with a girl. She was in as rough condition as he was. And my heart broke for them."[5]

Donna is the director and founder of The Healing of the Seven Generations, a non-profit organization that provides a space to connect and support Indigenous Peoples in the community, wherever they are in their journey. When she encounters community members in situations like Clarence's, she often begins by telling them about her own healing journey. Clarence listened and she quickly made an impression on him. He felt that there was something powerful in this woman.

Over the next few months, Clarence went back a few times to see Donna. She taught him about the history of Canada's relations with Indigenous Peoples, a history of failed attempts by colonizers to erase their existence. She taught him about the legacy of Canada's residential school system, and she explained how he himself was suffering from the intergenerational transmission of his ancestors' trauma. She explained how the Sixties Scoop was yet another instance of colonial aggression meant to erase indigeneity and assimilate Indigenous children into mainstream culture. She also started teaching him about his own Indigenous identity.

As she spoke to him, it became clear to Donna that Clarence was eager to learn. "He really absorbed all that," she says. It seemed to her that he really did want to get on a path of healing, that he was "sick and tired of being sick and tired." What Clarence lacked, however, was an ability to work through his shame, to let go of the crutches that addiction provided. Donna recollects that Clarence "didn't have any patience whatsoever. He wanted things to happen now... He was in a big hurry."

By 2009, eight years after he and Stephanie divorced, Clarence had worked for three different companies, been incarcerated once, and racked up several thousand dollars in by-law infractions — mostly for drinking in public.

> At that time in my life, I was in survival mode. I was not living. It was not life at all. It was a painful existence.

His lifestyle, his cycle of homelessness, was taking a toll on him, physically and emotionally. A well-known figure in downtown Kitchener, at St John's Kitchen, and House of Friendship's shelter, he was starting to feel the grind of the street.

> It was really painful. It was horrific. Wearing the same clothes for days in and days out, not being able to have a shower, not being able to change your underwear, not being able to do this, do that, it was hard.

Clarence was now drinking so heavily that he would sometimes black out and forget long stretches of time while inebriated. His heavy drinking also periodically caused paralyzing cramps throughout his whole body, the effect of prolonged dehydration. Many of his friends were leading high-risk lives, and some of them were having premature deaths. At the same time, Clarence was making connections with support workers who saw the humanity inside him, such as Donna Dubie and Jennifer Mains. Clarence also got to know a woman named Connie Hachborn who worked at the men's shelter. Over the years, as Clarence came in and out of that shelter, she got to know him in turn.

> It was a really cool thing because Connie, she didn't judge me. She accepted me for who I was. It didn't matter how dirty I looked, how broken I looked, how

smelly I looked... She talked to me and she was
starting to build a relationship with me.

In the fall of 2009, Connie asked Clarence if he would
consider going to a treatment centre for his addictions. She told
him about the process, about filling out an application form, and
getting ready to check into a detoxification centre.

Mentally, physically, spiritually, and emotionally I
was just done, and I was scared. I was also starting to
think there's more to life than the life I was leading.

He was thinking about being a helper and especially about his
daughters and his absence from their lives. It all started to add up,
the fear, the shame, the weariness.

One thing led to the next, and soon Clarence was at St Mary's
Counselling where his partner helped him fill out an application
form for a twenty-one-day program based out of a treatment centre
in Belleville, Ontario, about 300 km from Kitchener-Waterloo. It
was early October and the annual Oktoberfest celebrations would
kick off with the keg-tapping at Kitchener city hall. Before he left
for Belleville, Clarence had to detox at a local detoxification centre.
He made a deal with himself: no matter where he was, when that
keg was tapped, he would check into detox. Sure enough, on
October 9, 2009, after the crowd cheered at the keg-tapping, ready
to begin their drinking and partying, Clarence walked to Grand
River Withdrawal Management, a detoxification centre located
behind Grand River Hospital, to quit his drinking and partying.

What happened over the next few weeks is difficult for
Clarence to recall — "I had a wet brain." The hospital's records
indicate that he was admitted into withdrawal management three
times consecutively, from October 10-19, then again from October
20-30, and once again from November 4-6. His brief exits from the
detox centre were likely made in order to attend AA meetings.
While in treatment, Clarence also reconnected with his two

daughters. They were supportive of him but at the same time, they remained reserved: they had been burned too many times to let their guards down easily.

What Clarence does remember about his treatment was a hellish detoxification process. At least twice, nauseous and convulsing, Clarence was reduced to helplessness:

> I fell on my knees in the back room, praying to God or to the Creator or my higher power to take the craving and the obsession to drink away.

His body was experiencing withdrawal, the symptoms associated with sudden discontinued use of substances. Fortunately, prayer helped him make it through the worst of the symptoms: "It worked!" he recalls. His cravings passed. On November 6, 2009, Clarence emerged from detox, sober for the first time in roughly thirty years.

Four days later, he was waiting for a bus at Charles Street Terminal. His destination was Belleville where he was scheduled to do a twenty-one-day treatment program for his addictions. His partner waited with him.

> I remember while I was sitting there, I had some sleeping pills that I wanted to take with me because at that I was having a really hard time sleeping. But I lost the pills, and I can remember I was panicking sitting there waiting for the bus. I hopped on the bus anyways. I took the bus to Toronto and then from Toronto to Belleville.

When Clarence arrived in Belleville, he took a cab to the treatment centre, checked in and was shown to his room. In the morning, he discovered that there were fourteen other men in his cohort for the addiction treatment program. After filling out their paperwork, the men were given a tour. It was a large house with a portable classroom in the back parking lot. Staff served a filling breakfast and then explained the expectations for each day; it quickly became apparent to Clarence that this was not going to be like the summer camps he had attended as a child.

The plan for each day was very regimented. It started with exercise in the morning when everyone would walk down to the lake. Once back at the centre, they ate breakfast and started their chores, which would be checked by staff for satisfactory completion. During the day there were classes to attend in the portable:

> They'd pound us with the paperwork, the theory of addiction, relapse prevention, relationships, all this stuff. It was gruelling.

After three weeks, of the fourteen men who checked in, only four graduated. Clarence was one of them. He explains the secret to his success: "Keep your mouth shut, do the homework, make your bed, and mind your own business."

In the end, the "21-day, spin-dry program" was not very effective — perhaps not surprisingly. Clarence recalls its impact:

> I can remember going to one or two AA meetings in Belleville. I don't remember my time there that much; I just know I was there for the wrong reasons. When I got out, I found a guy downtown who was in the program, and I bought some weed from him. Hours after I left that program, I was getting high, because I wasn't there for myself.

This was November 2009. Clarence was forty-four years old. Within a few days he was back in Kitchener. He decided to continue to attend AA meetings, even finding a temporary sponsor, a man named George Passmore. Clarence managed to avoid alcohol for a couple of months, but he thought he could do it on his own. He never called George, never asked him for help. Eventually

Clarence stopped showing up to the meetings. Yet he still harboured his traumas and his shame.

> And then I was back out in the community doing more research (AA jargon for drinking again).

Before he went to Belleville, he had promised his daughters that he would sober up; he promised that he would be a better father. Now he drank down his promise, washing away his good intentions. He drank himself into another oblivion. "I know today that shame kills," he says. Over the next two months, Clarence found new depths of shame.

> I started drinking more heavily, started blacking out, started showing up at the hospital more frequently with full body cramps. I was dehydrated so much that I was having cramps throughout my whole body.

He was staying at House of Friendship's shelter again, meeting up with his friends at St John's Kitchen, dedicating each day to the pursuit of inebriation. February, March, and April of 2010 were months of the heaviest drinking in Clarence's life. But the poison took its toll, often resulting in trips to the hospital. In early April, after a serious bender, Clarence woke up in the hospital once again and realized with a terrifying clarity that, if he kept up this way, he was going to die.

Connie came to visit him.

"Have you hit your proverbial bottom, Clarence?" she asked. "Do you have a trapdoor down there?"

Abby Cachagee (1991)

*And I always had these huge flashbacks from the school,
from not being able to know what to expect. I was hurting
an awful lot and I had these horrid memories come back to
— I couldn't deal with them. Couldn't deal with them. I just
couldn't deal with them. So I said, "Well, I'm going to kill
myself." And I tried to kill myself. Didn't succeed on it.
They caught me and took me down to Toronto and gave me
[electric] shock treatment. And while in the hospital, for
some reason the shock treatment erased the raw of my bad
experiences. For many years I couldn't remember them. I
just felt good for a while.*

*And I noticed that as I was getting better from my shock
treatments, the person next door to me was getting worse.
He came in about the same time I did. And they take you
into this room. First they put you under. They'd grease up
your temples and you lay back. That's basically all I could
remember until I came out. And then when I came out of
the treatment there, I'd feel good. I'd feel a little stiff in the
jaw. Well, I, like you said, there was memories and feelings
and a lot of pain that I couldn't deal with. I felt that I didn't
want to go on. I didn't want to feel the same way again and
again, that there was no future.*

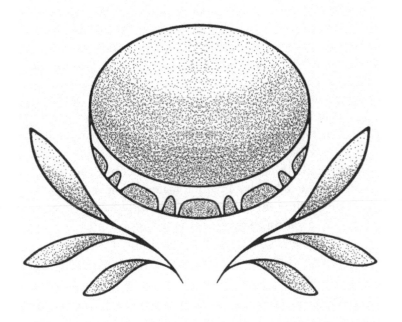

13

OUT OF THE BUBBLE

It's my understanding that when we sing with a Hand Drum, it's a form of prayer. It's an honour to sing for people, for communities, and for Creation. It keeps me connected to spirit, to culture, and to the natural things of Creation — because it was constructed with all natural material. I acknowledge the spirit of the drum. It's an honour to have a drum. There's also a responsibility in having a drum.

When you play or hear the drum, let it connect you to culture and Creation; let its beat resonate with you.

April 9, 2010 was Clarence's second time checking out of detox. He received his belongings, all he had to his name, from the nurse at the front desk: a knapsack with a change of clothes, some paperwork, a braid of sweetgrass, a pocketknife, and a half-full bottle of cologne,

> because I always had to smell good, regardless of how
> shitty I felt; they always said I was the best-dressed
> homeless guy in Kitchener-Waterloo.

A staff member teased that she considered keeping the sweet-grass for herself. Then they all wished him luck and he was off.

Two weeks earlier, Clarence had been staying at House of Friendship's shelter, downtown Kitchener. He had been drinking more heavily than ever in his life. Totally dehydrated, he would suddenly find himself incapacitated with full-body cramps. He was starting to experience blackouts; long stretches of inebriated existence vanished from his memory. Friends told him stories about his unremembered deeds, entire nights occupied by a doppelgänger — and a very unkind one if the reports were true. Waking up in the hospital one day, he realized a fearful truth: his alcohol addiction was about to destroy him.

> I didn't want to have a premature death. I knew that
> there was more to life than the life that I was leading.
> And I knew that I had a role and I had a responsi-
> bility to my daughters, and I had a role and responsi-
> bility to Creation. I didn't know what that was yet
> but I knew that I wanted to be a helper.

Clarence had told Connie, his friend and support worker, that he was ready to commit to healing and stay accountable; he was ready to go to any lengths to stay sober. His hands had trembled so much that he had needed her assistance filling out intake forms for the treatment centre. But how many times had Clarence said he was ready to change? How many promises had he made, only to be broken with another bender? He had disappointed a lot of his friends and family: the Reiers, his social workers, his ex-wife, his daughters. His previous efforts were futile, he explains now, because he never really meant it. He could not imagine a life that didn't include drugs and alcohol.

Now his life was on the line.

After they had filled out an Alcohol Drug Assessment Tool form, Clarence had had to pick which treatment centre to apply to. He wanted to stay close to his daughters, who were living in the Region of Waterloo, so he chose a treatment centre for men with addictions based out of Waterloo, operated by House of Friendship, and known simply by its address: One-Seventy-Four King.

On April 4, 2010, Clarence had his last drink with his friends.

> I was shaking so much and I was hurting so much, that one of my friends, he had some Methadone and he gave me a cap-full to calm me down.

After that, Clarence checked into detox.

> It was fucking brutal. They kept me in the bubble for two days and I had to beg them to let me out for the last day before I left for One-Seventy-Four. I was angry.

IT WAS a chilly morning in spring when Clarence checked out of the Grand River Withdrawal Management Centre with his knapsack on his shoulders. He walked northward up Park Street, behind the red-brick walls of the hospital, steam spewing from back vents; then he cut across a large parking lot to King Street, the main street that connects the two cities, Kitchener and Waterloo. The walk gave him plenty of time to ponder weighty thoughts.

> As I was getting closer, I kept thinking about my past, thinking about my childhood, thinking about my marriage, thinking about my daughters, thinking about my family, thinking about my foster family, thinking about all the friends that I had and all the

friends that I was leaving behind, and thinking about how hard this was going to be, and also thinking about how maybe this could really change my life.

Clarence had been here before, brief periods of white-knuckle sobriety — once after his marriage broke up, and then again after some friends intervened, and more recently while he attended a 21-day residential treatment program. But he had always relapsed at some point. He now explains that he was always doing it for someone else, for his ex-wife, for his friends, for his daughters. But this time something was different, and he was aware of it. He had chosen himself to do it; no one else was pushing him, advising him, or trying to fix him. But that didn't change the way his body felt. He was tired and achy from the withdrawal unit. He walked slowly to One-Seventy-Four King.

At some point travelling up King Street, one leaves the city of Kitchener and enters Waterloo. The two neighbouring cities long ago expanded and wove into one another. Clarence crossed over Union street and entered into Uptown Waterloo. On its south end, there is a large liquor store. As he walked past its wide, bright display windows, he wished his faithful friends farewell. Around this point, his pace noticeably slowed. The reality of his destination, and all of its consequences — if it were carried through to its logical end — suddenly bore down on him. A familiar instinct reared its head.

He stopped at the Tim Horton's on Spring Street, only a few blocks from the treatment centre, and entered into the bustle of a morning crowd, eagerly awaiting their routine fix of sugar and caffeine before heading off to work. How many of them were, like Clarence, contemplating the totality of their life at that moment? How many were on the brink of such fundamental transformation? As chance would have it, he ran into an old friend there, a man named Derek who happened to be himself currently enrolled at

One-Seventy-Four. Derek had some frightful news about another resident at the treatment centre:

> [Derek] says, "Hey what are you doin'?"
>
> I say, "I'm on my way to One-Seventy-Four."
>
> He says, "Oh, I'm there. Let me get you a coffee. But I want to tell you something first." He says, "Do you know Wayne?"
>
> I say, "Yeah, the guy from the [AA] meetings?"
>
> He goes, "Yeah." He says, "Wayne passed away in his sleep last night."

Wayne was a friend of Clarence who also struggled with addiction. He was seeking help and had checked into the treatment centre only a few weeks earlier. Quite unexpectedly, he suffered a fatal heart attack the night before, perhaps naturally or perhaps a bodily reaction to withdrawal.

It now seemed to Clarence that death loomed in all directions. Addiction was wreaking havoc on his body, revealed with incapacitating, full-body cramps, as well as the black outs. But sobering up was equally troubling: one of his friends who was trying to heal did not survive the withdrawal process. The stark reality of his Catch-22 became clear after Clarence left the cafe and rounded the corner of the block. A police car, an ambulance, and a coroner's vehicle were all parked in front of One-Seventy-Four. He thought, "Man, am I doing the right thing?" Something deep inside him repeated its well-versed chorus: *Run away!*

> But I managed to make it in there. I did my intake. They checked all my stuff. I got my room. We had a big meeting downstairs. They talked about Wayne passing away. While we were downstairs talking about it, they took Wayne's body out. Positive thing: he died sober. He was an alcoholic but he died sober.

ONE-SEVENTY-FOUR TRACES its origins to 1975 when House of Friendship purchased a building in Waterloo, leveraging grant money offered by the federal government for the establishment of new half-way houses. Its mandate was to help men who struggle with substance use by providing an alcohol-free environment for group and individual therapy, and common residence. The house has room for up to eleven residents, plus four who stay in a smaller house on their way out of the program. It is staffed from nine in the morning till five in the afternoon. If there's an emergency outside of staffed hours, residents can page a designated staff who is on-call.

Rick Pengalli, a counsellor at One-Seventy-Four, explains that new participants in the program first go through an assessment stage of one or two weeks.[1] If they are the right fit, they can decide to commit to the six- to eight-month program. New residents are assigned to one of two small groups, which meet twice a week for two hours. Cooking meals and upkeep of the house is the responsibility of the residents, and the chores are organized by an elected senior resident.

It is important to have formal meetings each week where the residents are encouraged to discuss living together in one common home. These are called Interpersonal Relationship groups (IPRs). "They start talking about their issues; they start talking about their stresses," Rick explains. In the meantime there are other groups and workshops on topics such as relationships, healthy masculinity, communication, and other positive life skills. Residents are also encouraged to attend AA or Narcotics Anonymous (NA) meetings outside of the program. A big component of group work is learning how to talk about feelings, emotions, and shame, learning how to use your voice.

Clarence had only been living at One-Seventy-Four for about two days when he suddenly felt as if everything around him was disintegrating. Reality started to wash over him. Once again,

Clarence felt the raw emotions of sobriety, normally washed away with whatever substance was available. It was an unbearable medley of shame, guilt, and self-disgust. He started to panic, wishing for his usual medication. He wanted to run. He went to the office of the counsellor on staff and banged on the door. "I need to talk to somebody. I need to talk to somebody right now!" he shouted.

Rick was on staff at the time; he answered the door and let Clarence into his office. Clarence recalls what happened next:

> I broke down. I started crying. I started weeping. I went right back to that scared little boy of about five maybe six years old, standing at the end of the lane with his suitcase, running away. I went right back to him.

Rick asked Clarence what he needed — what he needed at that moment to help him cope. Clarence said, "I need my sister. I want my sister here because I'm scared."

After taking some deep breaths, Clarence started to calm down. Rick describes his view of what happened during that interaction: "[Clarence] came into my office... and basically started to talk. He started telling me what he was going through and what was going on. He had to get real pretty quickly, emotionally real... I kind of look at it as the moment he made the commitment to himself that he was going to get better." After that, Rick became Clarence's one-on-one counsellor, and after several days in the treatment program, they decided that this was the right place for Clarence to be at this stage in his journey.

CLARENCE's first roommate at One-Seventy-Four was a man named Ted.[2] It was fitting that they shared a room because at the time Ted was on a path similar to Clarence's; he was trying to reconnect with his Indigenous identity through painting. They got along well and soon fell into a mutual routine.

> We'd go to our programs during the day, our small groups and one-on-ones, and then after Ted and I would go up to our room. He would start painting and I would start writing. I wanted to try to remember the times in my life, especially from the beginning.

Clarence filled notebooks with chicken-scratch entries, the nerves of his hands unruly from years of alcohol use, while Ted set up an easel by the window and painted elaborate and colourful pictures, filled with symbols and images. They were on the same path exploring different terrain. At first, Clarence wrote about his feelings and daily life at the centre, but over time the subject matter changed (and so did his penmanship). Old memories and stories started to seep onto the pages, remnants of a life ignored and forgotten in the immediacy of addiction and homelessness.

As he settled into the routine of the program, Clarence also started putting some of the pieces of his life back together.

> I was finally able to start addressing things that were lacking so long in my life. I started going to the dentist. I was seeing a doctor, Doctor Berrigan at the Kitchen. I became friends with him and started seeing him on a regular basis.

Meanwhile, Clarence got involved with an AA group that met nearby.

> When you're in the fellowship of AA, one of the first things you do is find a home group — that's a group that you stay accountable to — and you go to that group every week. You put your service hours in, if

that means helping to set up or helping to chair the group or greeting people at the door.

As he attended AA groups and small groups at One-Seventy-Four, Clarence found himself discussing things that had happened in his life which he had never discussed before.

> During that early time at One-Seventy-Four, I hadn't found my voice yet. When I did speak, I would get frustrated, or I would get scared, or I would get anxious, or I would get nervous, and then my voice would get all shaky and I thought people would judge me or stereotype me or make fun of me.
>
> The only time I would have a voice before was if I was under the influence of something. Drugs or alcohol would give me a voice. Sometimes it would make me a babbling fool, but other times I could carry on a half-decent conversation, as long as I was high or drinking — because I didn't have any confidence; I didn't have any self-esteem; I didn't know where I fit in, so I didn't feel like I had anything to contribute.

Using your voice is a common skill addressed at One-Seventy-Four. Group participants are encouraged to use I-statements, which express to others how actions impact them personally. But, as is often the case with self-help, learning the name of a new concept is not the same as putting it into practice. Clarence learned this quickly enough while living in close quarters with such a diverse group of individuals. Some of them inevitably pushed his buttons.

Twice each week, the men staying at the treatment centre met in their small groups, one upstairs and the other downstairs to discuss interpersonal relationships. These meetings were designed to provide a formal setting for the men to discuss any issues that had arisen between one another — the difficult stuff that comes out of life together in one big house. There was one meeting early on in which Clarence needed to air grievances about a new member to the household, one who Clarence felt was acting too entitled, too dismissive of the teachings and group activities, and too neglectful of the household tasks. Clarence spoke up with no intention of beating around the bush:

> I told him that the way he acted made me feel less-than, because it was like he felt entitled not doing the same jobs everyone else had to do. I said, 'I'm so frustrated with you and I've tried and tried and tried. I'm writing you off, so don't look at me, don't talk to me, don't acknowledge me.'

After that the counsellor Rick, who was facilitating the group, asked the man who had been singled out if this was the first time anybody had said something like that to him. "No." he replied, and that's all that he managed to say. After a period of silence, Rick suggested the group take a break. They dispersed for fresh air or for a smoke. When they got back together Rick restarted the session by giving the man who had been singled out another chance to speak. Rick describes what happened next: "The man started crying. He started talking about how this isn't the first time he's heard it, in fact he's heard it many times but he's never really listened. And his whole life has gone from being somebody who's had all kinds of money, had very good education, had an incredible family, and has thrown it all away. He felt completely alone."

Afterwards, Rick turned to Clarence and asked him if there was ever a time in his own life where someone had written him off. Clarence immediately understood. Yes, of course, countless times he himself had been ignored and given up on — he had also been written-off — and it had made him feel alone, scared, and sad. Clarence affirmed the honesty of the man he had singled out. They reconciled.

After it was all said and done, we made up and to this day we are still friends.

According to Clarence, as friends, now they can listen to each other and respectfully reply, "Yeah okay, but you're still full of shit."

Clarence explains that he was learning how to let those who bothered him help him grow. Rather than fixate on the aggravation, he would stop and take a step back, asking himself what it was about this person's behaviour that caused him to become upset. Was it because they were being mean? Or was it because they reminded him of something about himself that he didn't like? This was the inner work of maturity that he had neglected for so long, the lucid contemplation of truth within.

As Clarence became more invested in his AA group, he sought out a sponsor. "A sponsor is somebody who takes you through the steps of AA," Clarence explains. They are a committed member to an AA group.

They're there to give their opinion. And they're there to not co-sign on your bullshit.

Back during his first attempt at treatment, while attending AA groups in between detox and the residential program in Belleville, Clarence had found a temporary sponsor, George Passmore. But Clarence was not truly committed to healing then, so the sponsorship never became serious; he never actually took the time outside of group to do the inner work with George, to work through the steps.

Now that he was back in AA while at One-Seventy-Four, Clarence reconnected with George, but he was too embarrassed and shy to ask him to be his sponsor again. One month went by. Other residents started finding sponsors but Clarence still didn't have one. Finally, after one meeting, he worked up the courage to ask George out for coffee. Clarence recalls their conversation:

> So we go out for coffee and I'm there talking to George, doing some chit chat, some small talk about this and that, and then I said, 'George, you know what? I was wondering if you'd be willing to be my temporary sponsor?' Meanwhile I was going to ask him to be my sponsor but I was just too chicken-shit at the time. And then I said, 'No, George, just wait. Let me rephrase that.' I said, 'Will you be my sponsor? I'm looking for a sponsor in AA and I'd like you to be that person.'

George couldn't hold back a big smile. He was happy to be Clarence's sponsor. But he had a caveat: if they were going to do this, he wanted to do it right.

George said, "Clarence, are you willing to go to any lengths?"

Clarence said, "Yes."

"I want you at my place twice a week in the afternoons," George replied, "and bring your big book." (The big book is the nickname for the official book used by AA groups ever since the movement's inception in 1935.)

From then on, throughout the summer of 2010, twice a week in the afternoon, Clarence emerged from One-Seventy-Four with his backpack, and rode his bicycle to George's house on Park Street. They sat in his living room, George on his favourite chair and Clarence on the couch, and the two men read out loud together. When they started, Clarence hadn't read for a long time and he was still finding his voice.

> I was shy. I couldn't pronounce some of the words. I didn't know half of the words they'd use back then.

Every now and then Clarence stopped reading to look up a word in the dictionary. At first they read a few pages each afternoon, and then as Clarence grew more competent at reading, and started finding his voice, they read much more than a few pages.

> It got me reading again. It got me communicating, talking about things. It got my mind working again.

As Clarence started using his voice more clearly, friends and counsellors began to encourage him to tell his story. Additionally, he was inspired by the support he was getting from his friend and sponsor, George. He wanted to give back, to pay it forward.

> That's when I knew that I wanted to become a helper. I also think that there were so many people that helped me along the way that I wanted to start giving back and being one of those helpers. You know what I mean? But to be a helper, it meant that you had to walk with integrity.

❧

It happens every other year. At One-Seventy-Four the staff organize a canoe trip in Massasauga Provincial Park, near Parry Sound on the east coast of Georgian Bay, about a four-hour drive north from Kitchener. They invite a mixture of residents who are currently at the centre and alumni. Space was limited with only six canoes, and since he was one of the newer residents, Clarence wasn't given priority to be included on the trip. However, it turned out that one of the alumni was unable to join, so a week before departure, Clarence was asked if he would like to fill the empty spot. He agreed and quickly arranged with a roommate to make sure his belongings were delivered to his daughters in case something happened to him — slightly overestimating the danger of such a trip. "Reflecting back on this time, fear of the unknown had immeasurable power over me," he journaled later.

Massasauga Park consists of hundreds of islands carved out by an equal number of inland lakes and rivers across 130 square kilometres. Twelve men were part of the adventure that year: two staff members, two alumni, and eight current residents. Their trip would involve three days of canoeing, with two nights spent camping on islands throughout the park. Clarence journaled:

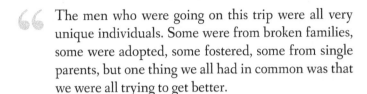

> The men who were going on this trip were all very unique individuals. Some were from broken families, some were adopted, some fostered, some from single parents, but one thing we all had in common was that we were all trying to get better.

There was a shared excitement throughout the treatment centre leading up to departure day. Those involved were getting supplies ready, packing warm clothes for the chilly April weather, and making lists of gear they would need. When the day came, staff carefully tied down all the canoes to three vehicles. Everyone packed in and they were off. On their way, Clarence carefully studied the alumni who had joined the trip, trying to determine what was different about them, asking himself what made them special? Why were they able to overcome their addictions, unlike so many others?

Staff members ascertained everyone's experience level and arranged teams accordingly. When they arrived at the lake, the group gathered on the shore to discuss water safety and the day's itinerary, which included approximately three hours of paddling. It was a damp, overcast day with moderate winds. Some of the men looked at the high swells and promptly concluded that the waves were too big for canoes. Rick, a counsellor from One-Seventy-Four, reassured them, saying, "Yes, but that's part of going canoeing. You start off with something scary and you never know exactly where you're going to go." One of the main reasons staff at One-Seventy-Four organize these trips is because they always prove to be such good teaching tools. There are always unforeseen challenges out on the water, and the only way to survive is to work through challenges together.

They split into three canoes and launched their packed vessels into the choppy lake. Clarence remembers that moment:

> In my canoe, two of the three had limited experience
> and it showed. It took us a while to get our bearings,
> but in time we caught up to the others. It seemed we
> were going everywhere except the direction we
> needed.

In time they grew accustomed to proper technique.

> The paddle was an extension of our body, and when
> we were in sync it was surprising how much distance
> we could cover.

As soon as they entered the park, he found himself in awe of
the world around him:

> I would focus on paddling and then look around and
> be consumed by the beauty that Creation had to
> offer. Being in nature and the outdoors always
> brought a certain peace to me. In my youth I was
> always exploring in the fields, streams, forests, and
> found myself connected while never feeling alone.

After a few hours of canoeing, Clarence felt the strain of work
in his body. His knees were aching and his back complained. His
mind wandered, reflecting on family, relationships, and recovery.
He caught his reflection in the black lake and contemplated its
deep unknown, wondering if such murky water was suitable for
fishing. They paddled quietly through the weaving rivers and slid
past silent islands. His knuckles began to blister. The refrain from
an old camp song came to his mind:

...dip, dip, and swing,
dip, dip, and swing...

The wind was relentless during the first stretch. Everyone kept asking Rick how much further it was to the campsite. "Oh, just around the bend," he kept saying with a grin. Quite a few bends later, an exhausted crew landed on a rugged shore strewn with patches of trees and grass and mossy points that jutted out into the lake. It was still windy and cold, and periodically it rained. They delegated tasks and then went to work setting up camp and helping to prepare dinner. After dinner, Clarence borrowed someone's disposable camera and began to explore the island, losing himself to the temporary home — a small patch of earth housing an eclectic group for the day. Time slipped away as Clarence became engrossed in the unfolding beauty of it all.

While wandering along the shore of the island, something caught his eye, a white spot on a peak of exposed bedrock. He carefully climbed across the rocks and discovered that it was a turtle shell, about the size of his fist, bleached white-grey by prolonged exposure to the elements. He picked it up and studied the small remnant of life. When he came back to the campsite, he showed the shell to Rick. Clarence recalls:

> 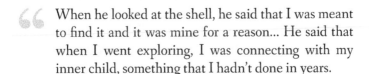 When he looked at the shell, he said that I was meant to find it and it was mine for a reason... He said that when I went exploring, I was connecting with my inner child, something that I hadn't done in years.

Rick remembered that moment too. "It was just like watching a little kid discover something but who had never been allowed to keep things, and now he was able to." Rick feels that at that moment Clarence was learning how to be a part of something bigger than himself.

Around the campfire that evening, the men shared stories, but once the sun set, it didn't take long for the weary travellers to retire to their tents. The first night was a chilly one. One man in Clarence's tent complained of the cold all through the night. Another claimed to hear noises outside and saw bear-shaped shadows in the dark. "That set the tone for an uneasy sleep,"

Clarence journaled. In the morning he was the first to rise, and he listened to the ghostly call of the loons as he built up the fire, reminding him of his visits to Fox Lake Reserve. After breakfast the campers repacked their supplies and set off for day two of the trip.

Day two was a longer stretch than the first. It included a section exposed to the open bay. Rick had warned everyone that this would require more diligence because of the larger swells in the open water. After an hour of canoeing, they stopped at a peninsula, just around the bend was Georgian Bay. One paddler accosted a passing boater to ascertain the size of the waves. "Oh, they're big," the boater warned, which quickly put everyone on edge. Then, as they prepared to leave the shore, one man stood up in his canoe while another was seated at the bow. In an instant, the canoe capsized, sending both of them and all of their supplies into the frigid waters. The team helped gather the supplies and drag the canoe to shore where they emptied it out. The men who took the plunge were not in the best spirits after that, to say the least. Clarence couldn't help but smile at the whole ordeal. After drying off as much as possible, they finally entered the open water:

> The bay was covered in whitecaps, the wind was strong, and it made paddling very tiring. The second day brought many aches and pains, and I didn't have as much gas in my tank as the previous day.

Luckily, they were heading directly into the wind, as opposed to having to navigate a cross-wind, so with a little perseverance, they made it across without losing too much time. The campsite wasn't much farther but it had started to rain. Rick describes the relief they felt when they arrived at that second campsite: "The sun had come out. The wind died. It was beautiful. We were on an island where everybody was cooking and just feeling good about themselves ... One of the staff started cooking steaks."

That night, the men shared stories and made S'mores. No one complained about the cold. They all slept soundly, exhausted and content to have a dry place to lay their heads. There was no rain in the morning and Clarence was the first to rise once again. "By the third day we were all a little sore, damp, tired, and smelling like the bush," he wrote. But the skies cleared, and it was smooth sailing back to the boat launch.

> Reflecting back on this experience, it was a contributing factor of my wellness journey. In those early days of my recovery, I was fortunate to be connected to a power greater than myself. I was able to feel the connection to a community, a sense of belonging that gave me purpose to go on.

Clarence brought the turtle shell he found with him back to Kitchener.

ABOUT FIVE MONTHS into his stay at One-Seventy-Four, Clarence was participating in a Sharing Circle at the centre. One man in the circle started to share his own experience using drugs. The man's vivid descriptions triggered Clarence, whose mind began to race. The counsellor in session noticed Clarence had disengaged — his eyes were closed and he was breathing deeply. She stopped the circle and checked in with him. Clarence said he needed a break, and he went back to his place. He tried eating. He tried watching TV. He tried reading. Nothing worked. His mind wouldn't stop racing through thoughts of drugs, alcohol, shame, cravings. He went out onto the porch of his house, into the hot summer day.

> I prayed to God. I prayed to the Creator. I said, 'If you're there, hear me and help me to calm my mind.'

After praying, Clarence opened his eyes to the dance of maple leaves in a summer breeze. Then, out of his peripheral vision, a butterfly fluttered into full view and perched on a branch in the tree in front of him, slowly opening and closing her wings.

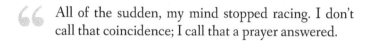

> All of the sudden, my mind stopped racing. I don't call that coincidence; I call that a prayer answered.
>
> I can remember at One-Seventy-Four when I was finding my higher power, when I was getting in contact with my inner child, when I was finding my voice, when I was challenging myself, when I was reprogramming myself, I was also on a quest to reconnect with my culture and my heritage. And I had to do this on my own.

CLARENCE TRACES his path to spirituality to when he first met his biological parents, especially his father, who taught him about his Indigenous identity. "I think that ignited a flame inside of me," he recalls.

> While I was in that treatment centre, I also started reconnecting with the Native centres that were in this community. I wanted to try to reconnect with my culture and heritage, and I knew that because my family was so far up north, I would have to reach out to some of the local agencies within the community, in Kitchener-Waterloo.

Clarence had connected with local Indigenous resources before his treatment, such as The Healing of the Seven Generations. So he returned to visit Donna Dubie, eager to start exploring his Indigenous identity. She was elated to hear about the work he was doing and soon introduced him to a cultural advisor at the centre, Gerard Sagassige, who is from Curve Lake First Nation.

Clarence asked for help learning. "Well, if I teach you, you need to start at the bottom," Gerard said. "You can't start halfway up the ladder. You need to start at the bottom and work your way up so you don't miss anything." Clarence explains:

> Gerard started talking to me about culture, about tradition, about ceremonies, about teachings, about the medicines and all these things. It felt good. It was like I was a sponge, and I was absorbing all of these things. They were teaching me about Protocol, about how to approach, how to ask, how to be grateful, how to be humble.

At one point Clarence showed Gerard the turtle shell he had found while on the canoe trip at Massasauga Park. Gerard looked at it and said, "I would be honoured if you let me turn that into a shaker for you." Clarence agreed, and when Gerard gave it back to Clarence, the new turtle shaker would later become the first sacred object that would make up his healing bundle. Noticing Clarence's enthusiasm for his Indigenous heritage, Donna suggested that, after he had completed his treatment at One-Seventy-Four, he enrol into Native Horizons, an Indigenous treatment centre located on the Mississaugas of the Credit First Nation Reserve.

In October 2010, Clarence graduated from One-Seventy-Four. Staff held a ceremony in the basement. Clarence invited friends and family to come celebrate with his favourite dessert, cherry cheesecake.

> That's what Eileen used to make really well. You can't duplicate that stuff when it's made with love.

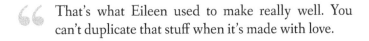

At least thirty people were there, including social workers and friends.

> And my half-brother Asher was there. My sister Cheryl was there. My daughters were there. Madison was crying; she was so emotional. Carleigh said, 'Thank you for giving my dad back to us.' Cheryl said, 'Thank you for giving my brother back.'

Clarence was so overwhelmed he now forgets much of what he said that day.

> I thanked One-Seventy-Four and everybody there for investing in me and letting me be me.

Abby Cachagee (1991)

But getting back, the school never gave you the tools. They never gave the information on how to handle things. It was later, much later, I went into a Native alcohol treatment program. And prior to going into Native alcohol treatment program, every time I would see a Native person drunk on the street I would walk across the road. I would never call myself an Indian. I spent two and a half years in the United States. I was an Italian, I was a Mexican, I was South American, but I was never an Indian. I just said I'm not that. I was somebody else.

But in that alcohol treatment program, the Native program, it gave me information, it gave me an identity, it gave me background. It told me who I was. It told me what an Indian was. I never knew what an Indian was before. I never knew what the history was, what the practices were.

14

RECONNECTING

Sunday November 7, 2010, eleven days after graduating from One-Seventy-Four, Clarence was on his way to Native Horizons, a treatment centre that specializes in Indigenous healing practices and Trauma Release Therapy. The centre is located on the Mississaugas of the Credit Reserve, which is just beside Six Nations of the Grand River. The six-week program treats a co-ed cohort of up to sixteen community members. After meeting his new roommate and unpacking his belongings, Clarence journaled:

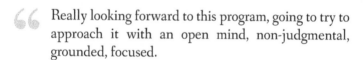 Really looking forward to this program, going to try to approach it with an open mind, non-judgmental, grounded, focused.

For their first group activity, the staff gathered the new participants in a large room. They asked that anyone who didn't grow up with their biological parents move across to the other side. Everyone in the room moved over to the other side. Then the staff asked that anyone who didn't finish high school move again to the other side. Everyone moved back. This back and forth repeated itself, and without fail almost all of the group went from one side to the other.

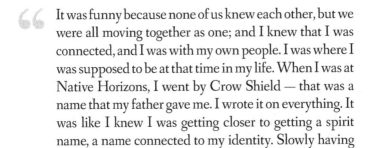

> It was funny because none of us knew each other, but we were all moving together as one; and I knew that I was connected, and I was with my own people. I was where I was supposed to be at that time in my life. When I was at Native Horizons, I went by Crow Shield — that was a name that my father gave me. I wrote it on everything. It was like I knew I was getting closer to getting a spirit name, a name connected to my identity. Slowly having exposure to prayer, medicine, teachings, meditations, I was starting to do spirit work, and my spirit was yearning for a name. I resonated with Crow Shield.

On the second day at Native Horizons, Clarence got up at 6:40 a.m. to go for a morning walk in the brisk fall weather. After breakfast, he attended a workshop on relationships and communication — important skills to have when living with strangers for six weeks. That afternoon, there was an AA meeting in which the participants heard from two graduates of the program. Clarence was impressed with the way each speaker shared from the heart not the head, as he puts it. Each day participants smudged and read meditations.

> We would all lay down, or close our eyes, and the Program Cultural Team Lead would tell us a story or play a flute. It was a guided meditation, but you were also getting a teaching at the same time. It was all new to me; I was used to mainstream treatment centres: paperwork, the theory and mind, and relapse prevention, and all that stuff, but at Native Horizons they actually connected with your spirit. They were starting to show us routine, starting to put structure

back into our lives. We were also practising medita-
tion and deep breathing.

A guest teacher visited and taught participants how to make
deer-hide drums. "That was where I made my first drum," recalls
Clarence.

> I can remember an Elder would come talk to us in the
> evenings — Grandmother Renee Thomas-Hill,
> Mohawk from Six Nations — she would come in and
> give us teachings. She was very kind and gentle; she
> would share teachings and tell us stories.

All participants in the treatment program at Native Horizons
are assigned chores while in residence. For the first week, Clarence
was on dish duty with two others. As is so often the case with doing
the dishes, by the second day it had already brought out conflicting
personality types. Clarence perceived that it was only himself and
one other who were taking on the brunt of the work, which made
him feel disrespected.

> When I grew up with the Reiers, we all had certain
> jobs and certain roles. Cheryl and I did the dishes,
> one dried and one washed. We'd complain. We'd joke
> around a little bit. But we had to do it.

Clarence asked the third person assigned to dishes if he
planned to do his job this time. Apparently his approach was too
blunt because the man flung a sink strainer at him and stormed out
of the kitchen. The next morning staff helped facilitate a conversation and the two worked it out.

Over the next few weeks at Native Horizons, every day was
chock full of activities: group counselling, workshops, film screen-
ings, meal preparation, and, of course, socializing. The first week
Clarence had classes on healthy eating and medicinal foods. There

was also an AA group and a Narcotics Anonymous (NA) group that met weekly. Clarence attended both. Guest speakers visited to give presentations, often personal stories of resilience. At the end of the first week, to have a break from all the heavy emotional work, the staff took everyone to a glow-in-the-dark mini putting course. That evening Clarence journaled:

> Have really been getting a lot out of the program, starting to dig at my inner self where most of my problem lies.

By Monday of the second week, three participants had already left the program; it was proving too demanding for where they were at on their journey. Clarence wished them well as they left. He was fortunate to have built some of his foundation already while in treatment at One-Seventy-Four. But One-Seventy-Four was a mainstream treatment facility, and as such it had not been able to explore a critical part of Clarence's identity. It was missing the Indigenous part of the picture. One-Seventy-Four also didn't work on trauma.

> They actually helped me figure out what my core issues were, but they couldn't help with trauma-related therapy.

Early Friday morning of the second week, staff sent the men to set up the Sweat Lodge located at the back of the premises to prepare for a Sweat Lodge ceremony. Clarence explains its significance:

> The Sweat Lodge represents the womb of Mother Earth.[1] You go in there to pray. You go in there to connect with the Creator, with the Ancestors. You call the Ancestors in. You call your Spirit Helpers in. It's a purification ceremony.

In the afternoon, one of the counsellors led the participants in the ceremony, which can become very intense, emotionally, physically, and spiritually. Clarence says that often while in the Sweat Lodge people will sing together or weep together.

> It is there to purify you, to pull that stuff out that you've been harbouring inside for such a long time.

After undergoing four rounds inside the Lodge, Clarence went back to his dormitory completely exhausted. He journaled:

> Was my second Sweat ever and the heat was very overpowering, but also very comforting. Was an amazing experience, something that I always wanted to be a part of.

In addition to traditional ceremonies, group sharing, and educational workshops, there was also a lot of hands-on work at Native Horizons. Participants were taught how to create certain Indigenous sacred items, such as drums, shakers, or tobacco pouches. The counsellors also assigned homework. For their first written assignment, after a workshop on the lasting impact of shame and guilt, participants were asked to write down a personal experience that had caused these feelings. Outdoors that evening, sitting around the campfire, everyone took a turn placing into the flames their memories of shame and guilt.

Clarence had heard from past graduates of Native Horizons that during the fifth week the going gets truly rough. One of the most challenging activities is called the Lifeline. This is a technique of Trauma Release Therapy that involves writing out a chronology of one's life, noting and acknowledging all the impactful events throughout, and then revisiting those traumatic events with the aid of counsellors and in the presence of the group. For Clarence, this meant he had to go back to those traumas he had buried down and neglected for so long. There were two that still had an especially strong hold over him: his abandonment as a child and the sexual abuse he experienced at a young age in Toronto.

After writing his Lifeline on Monday, Clarence journaled:

> I feel drained from all the mental memories, emotions, discomfort. I know that this is something that I've needed to do for a very long time. Pain comes first before healing can take place. Lived long enough with this pain.

In the second part of the Lifeline assignment, participants share what they wrote with the group. As he listened to others share, Clarence was impressed with their courage. He could often relate to the past experiences of others, especially when one man shared about his interaction with Children's Aid Society. Clarence journaled: "Feel a lot of shame when I hear the letters C.A.S. Very negative time in my life."

As each day passed, he started to become anxious about sharing his own Lifeline:

> Have been carrying this fucking stuff *too long*!!

At the end of the week, it was Clarence's turn to share; he was the last person to share his Lifeline. Two counsellors accompanied him into a small room with two large sheets of paper on the wall; written on them were the two traumas Clarence wished to overcome. His fellow residents were seated around the perimeter. Lying down in the centre of the room, coached by two counsellors at his side, he started at the beginning.

> It was a process where they would coach you back; 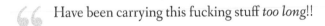 they would put you into a deep breathing exercise. They would tell you to envision yourself at a young age. They would tell you to envision yourself at the age you are now, standing there holding hands with

yourself at a young age. And then while the both of you are standing there, they asked you to envision a bright light around you. With that image, you were supposed to slowly shrink it down. Shrink it down. Shrink it down until it could fit into the palm of your hands. When that vision was small enough, you were supposed to take that and put it to your heart. And that's when the process started; and then they would start taking you back to those traumatic times in your life.

I was able to go back deep inside of me with my inner child, pull those traumatic times out of my life, face them, and release them. I forgave my parents for the abandonment, and I forgave those men who abused me. And it was like a weight was lifted.

That evening, he journaled:

> Had some very positive feedback from the others. Really starting to like the man I'm becoming.

That weekend, his sister Cheryl picked him up, and they visited some family near Toronto and then attended a Pow-Wow in Hamilton. During that week, Clarence continued to learn about himself through Indigenous teachings. One day he wrote a letter to his biological parents, asking why they had abandoned him as a child, explaining how it made him feel all those years. He also began to work on the Eighth step of AA: righting all the wrongs done to others in the midst of addiction. There were twenty people on Clarence's list. He probably could have written many more.

The rest of his time at Native Horizons consisted of more teachings, more Sweats, making more sacred items, and gaining more wisdom. He also heard about an intriguing post-secondary program: the Native Community Worker diploma offered by Anishinabek Educational Institute, which was an hour's drive north of Kitchener-Waterloo. He had been thinking about pursuing a career as a helper, and an education in the counselling field seemed like a natural next step.

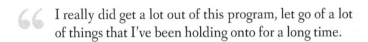 I really did get a lot out of this program, let go of a lot of things that I've been holding onto for a long time.

By his final week in Native Horizons, snow was just starting to cover the ground. He graduated December 17, 2010.

Soon after coming back to Kitchener, Clarence went to visit his friend and mentor Donna Dubie. She told him about a culturally-based, Healing Lodge called Kiikeewanniikaan, located on the Munsee-Delaware Nation Reserve, which is about 140 kilometres southwest of Kitchener. "It would be like putting the icing on the cake," said Donna. This treatment program was only two weeks long. Even though Clarence had just been through two different addiction treatment programs, he was eager to learn more about Indigenous culture and teachings.

After a brief holiday, on Sunday, January 9, 2011, Clarence made his way to Delaware-Munsee Nation for a two-week stay at Kiikeewanniikaan (Kiikee). Like Native Horizons, Kiikeewanniikaan also used a mixture of Trauma Release Therapy and culturally-based practices in its treatment program. The centre of the building was a large gathering place. Radiating out from the centre were four wings for families, single men, single women, and staff.

At Kiikee, Clarence continued to learn about himself and others. There were many Indigenous teachings and ceremonies. For instance, he heard one Elder tell the Creation story with a rendition so detailed that it consisted of two morning sessions. There were Sweat Lodge ceremonies and feet soaks in warm water with sea salt and peppermint (accompanied by cedar tea).

Had Clarence been raised in an Anishinaabe community, he would likely have received a spirit name as he grew into adulthood.

⚛

A SPIRIT NAME is a name that is gifted to you through ceremony.[2] And only certain people have the gift of gifting names. The individual who has the gift will pray and think and then the name will come to them that suits the individual who is asking.

> It was something that really helped solidify who I was in regards to identity.

Clarence felt fortunate to spend time among so many Elders while at Kiikee. He connected with one in particular:

> There was one Elder there, Peter Linkletter (Pathfinder). He was a Vietnam vet. He was an ex-heroin addict... He was really cool.

Peter was also the conductor of Sweat Lodge ceremonies at the treatment centre. Nervously, one day Clarence asked Peter if he would gift him with a spirit name. Peter said that a spirit name is unpredictable but that he would keep it in mind.

Much of Clarence's time at Kiikee was spent in group therapy or workshop sessions. Participants explored concepts such as grief, love, honesty, acceptance, or trust. In a Sharing Circle focused on grief, Clarence journaled afterward about his abandonment issues:

> For so long [I] have been trying to free the ghost that hides in my soul, the ghost of abandonment.

Like Native Horizons, participants at Kiikee were encouraged to write their own personal Lifeline, although in this case each person was supposed to write two: one that focused on struggles throughout life, and one that focused on the positive events. As Clarence carefully examined his life once again, he realized that love was a difficult thing for him to come to terms with, in the past and presently. When he shared his Lifeline with the group, he disclosed how for a good portion of life he had equated sex with love, thinking that the more sex he had, the closer he would get to love.

Afterwards one of the Elders had a conversation with Clarence and encouraged him to address the negative ways he had treated women in the past. He suggested that Clarence write a letter that explored the way that he had been thinking about love and how he understands it now. He journaled:

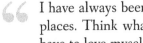

> I have always been looking for love in all the wrong places. Think what it really boils down to is: I first have to love myself and then I can really start to feel and appreciate love as a whole.

It was a cold, windy afternoon in mid-January — the heart of winter. A large white passenger van pulled to the side of the road near the Highway Nine bridge over the Thames River, known to the Anishinaabe as the Askunessippi, "the antlered river." Ten individuals stepped out of the van, wrapped in winter jackets and thick scarves. They walked down the road to the bridge and lined up along its metal guard rails. Few words were spoken as the chilly breeze welled up tears in their eyes — for some it was not just the wind. Down below the Thames River had avoided freezing in its two-hundred-kilometre rush to Lake Saint Clair. Ice gathered along the shore, but in the unfrozen middle was a deep darkness.

Each person held a small tie of tobacco in their hands that they had created earlier that day. Into each, they had imparted their griefs and resentments.

"The water is medicine," someone said. "It will heal those negative times in your life. After you drop your ties into the water, don't look back."

Like flower petals, ten red tobacco ties fell down to the surface of the stream, where they were whisked away in an instant, carried to a place unknown, burdens accepted without a ripple of protest. Ten individuals walked back to the van, each a little lighter on their healing journey.

At Kiikee and Native Horizons, the way Clarence perceived the world slowly started to change:

> I started looking at life through a different lens. And that was through the help of the teachings, that was through the help of the Elders giving us stories, that was through the help of working with the medicines, that was through the help of doing the ceremonies, being exposed to Sweats and knowing what a Sweat is.

It was during the second Sweat Lodge ceremony, that Peter/Pathfinder received a spirit name for Clarence:

ᑭᐊᐧᑊ ᑎᓈᐧᑊ ᐃᐧᓂᐟ

North Wind Man

> It's funny because I love the winter. My whole life I've been really connected to the winter. I think there's nothing better than feeling that cold north wind blowing on your face, where it's so fresh, and you go outside after the snow and everything's pure and white. I was always connected to the winter, so I think it's pretty awesome that that name is connected to me.

Abby Cachagee (1991)

The thing that was lacking, I believe, in all the residential schools was the lack of a role model.

We never had a role model. There was nobody there we could look up to and say, "I would like to be that person. This person knows how to do this, do that."

There was no one around. The only role model you had were the older students. And a lot of times that type of model was very negative. Very negative.

15

BECOMING A HELPER

> After I came back from the Healing Lodge and I
> transitioned back into this community, I started pray-
> ing. I didn't know how to pray but I started praying. I
> started smudging every day.

After graduating from Kiikeewanniikaan in February 2011,
Clarence had a sense of what he wanted to do moving
forward.

> I was so grateful for the life that was given to me. I
> wanted to give something back to Creation.

After he left One-Seventy-Four, Clarence moved into a
Waterloo apartment that was subsidized through Supportive
Housing of Waterloo (SHOW), a living arrangement he was very
thankful for.

> SHOW gave me a sanctuary and a foundation to start building on, in order to find purpose, meaning, and direction.

Now his plan was twofold: he wanted to become more involved in his community by volunteering and he wanted to continue learning about his culture and identity. He made sure to keep in touch with friends at The Healing of the Seven Generations, as well as other Indigenous organizations in the region.

> I was looking for a teacher. It's hard to be patient. It's hard to work on yourself and be patient and wait for those right people to come into your life who are going to give you those things that are missing — ceremonies, teachings, stories, songs — all of these things that help a man to have a good heart and a good mind.

He also went to see an old friend, Jennifer Mains, the coordinator at St John's Kitchen. He asked her if he could start volunteering at the Kitchen. She was receptive of the idea and brought it up at the next staff meeting. The staff agreed that Clarence would be a good fit, and in March he started volunteering three days a week.

> My job was to serve the people, work the floor, and make myself available to everybody who was there. And it was good. It made me feel good to come back and serve in the community. I felt pretty humbled to be able to come back and work in that element.

Jennifer was grateful to have Clarence helping. She recalls that "Clarence brought a gentleness to the Kitchen and a respect for the place, and an understanding of the culture." Having lived experience of addictions and homelessness, Clarence had a knack for supporting people going through similar struggles because he could often relate to what they were feeling. But, at the same time, having a past at the Kitchen could sometimes complicate old relationships. Many of his friends that he used to drink with still came to the Kitchen.

> I remember when I would see some of my old friends. They would say, 'Clarence, good for you, buddy, but for me it's too late.' I would always say, 'I'm paving the way for you guys.'
>
> But it's never too late. What if I would have said it's too late? It's never too late to have hope. It's never too late to heal. It's never too late to forgive. It's never too late to love.

Clarence still considered them his friends, and they were certainly supportive of him, but he could no longer condone everything they were up to. He did his best to stay respectful and be straight with everyone there.

> In that Kitchen everybody's equal and we don't judge. We don't stereotype.

It was also a time of intense learning for Clarence. Helping people fill out forms, find housing, and access community resources prepared him for future employment in the field. He was even invited to participate in staff meetings:

> It was nice to sit in on their meetings and see how it all went down, see how it works. Jennifer would ask me for my perspective, for my views on certain situations or certain incidents. It was pretty cool.

In the meantime, Clarence had to work on putting his life back together.

> I started clearing up the wreckage of my past. I
> started making amends and taking care of some busi-
> ness that I had avoided for such a long time. I went
> back into family court, and I dealt with that, which
> was one of the most stressful times in my life.

During his time in treatment, Clarence had fallen several thousand dollars behind in child support. So, while he was still volunteering at the Kitchen and doing his best to support people there,
he was also being supported himself by an outreach worker and
friend, Stuart Dunbar. They went together to family court to work
out an arrangement to pay his arrears.

After that first court appearance, Clarence walked out of the
courthouse on Frederick Street and made his way over to the bus
terminal. When he arrived, he leaned against the cement walls.

> The judge called me a deadbeat dad. He said, 'If I
> could lock you up, I would.' He made me feel like the
> lowest of the low. I shut down at the stand. I just
> disconnected, didn't say anything.

Waiting for his bus after his court appearance, Clarence
thought to himself, "How nice would a shot of rye be right now?"
He wanted to give up.

> If there was any time in my sobriety that I was
> pushed to the limit, that was the time.

But this time he had the tools. He had a support network,
friends who reassured him and kept him accountable.

> My friend Stuart was there the whole time, and he
> did a lot of work. I'm very grateful that he was there,
> and that he did that for me.

Clarence began looking for paid work. He needed to start making payments to his family. He also wanted to stay occupied.

> It was a crazy time in my life because I was early in recovery and I thought I had to stay busy. Staying busy would keep my mind off of things and it would help me find direction. From 2011 to 2013 I had like five jobs. Just go, go, go, go, go!

His first job was a part-time position as a Peer Health Worker based out of the Kitchener Downtown Community Health Centre. He was tasked with building relationships with men in the community who were falling through the cracks of the social service system.

> You would talk to the men there and you would form a relationship with them as best as you could. And then you would let them know what supports were available in the community. It was my job to help these individuals navigate the system.

Because he himself was in recovery for addictions, sometimes Clarence made strong connections with the people he was working with. He could relate to their struggles. On the other hand, some people felt uncomfortable speaking with him. It could be shameful to talk to someone who had seemingly overcome a struggle that they could not. So Clarence had to learn how to adapt his support based on where people were at in their recovery journey — it wasn't a one-size-fits-all approach. And he clearly excelled because he was recognized with the "Kindred Spirit Award," in 2014, an award sponsored by a network of social services in downtown Kitchener that recognizes the work of a helper who has lived experience of homelessness.[1]

Clarence holding the Kindred Spirit Award

At the same time, Clarence had education on his mind: a social work diploma offered by the Anishinabek Education Institute (AEI) called 'Social Service Worker with Indigenous Knowledge', which he heard about back when he was at Native Horizons. It sounded right up his alley. But before he could go to college, he needed to get his high school diploma, so he enrolled at the St Louis Adult Learning Centre in downtown Kitchener.

In March 2011, Clarence walked down King Street from his apartment in Waterloo, making his way to downtown Kitchener. "I always used to walk a lot back then," he recalls, mentioning that the time it took to walk from his apartment in Waterloo to downtown Kitchener was more than an hour. Three blocks away from St Louis Adult Learning Centre, he started feeling anxious. It had been almost thirty years since he dropped out of grade eleven in 1982.

 I could feel my old negative core beliefs starting to come in — that I'm not good enough, that I'm not worthy — and I wanted to run. But because I had these tools that I learned in the treatment centres I was able to stop. I was able to process it. I was able to sit in those feelings. Instead of running, I was able to challenge those feelings. I said, 'Clarence, you could either run like you've always done, or you could stay accountable to this commitment and do whatever it takes to get there and to get your grade twelve.'

He walked through the doors of the building.

Three months later, after a lot of hard work, he walked out, high school diploma in hand. Clarence's job as a Peer Health Worker was only seven and a half hours a week. It worked well while he was getting his diploma, but as he got closer to graduation, he started looking for more employment. His search led him to begin another job at House of Friendship in the Men's Shelter on Charles Street as a relief worker for the shelter, the same shelter he had stayed at periodically in the past.

Soon after that, he was hired by The Working Centre for another part-time position. Within a few months, Clarence was working five part-time jobs: peer health worker at the Kitchener Downtown Community Health Centre, on call housing worker and tenant support worker at The Working Centre, outreach worker at St John's Kitchen, and relief staff hostel support worker at House of Friendship. "Sunday was my only day of rest," he admits.

While working in the social service sector, Clarence was also finding his voice through various speaking engagements:

> I was speaking at universities. I was speaking at colleges. I was speaking at schools. I can remember the first time that it was hard because I had to step outside of my comfort zone once again.

When Clarence began the two-year Social Service Worker diploma at AEI in September 2012, he already had experience in social work. The program, a partnership between the AEI and Loyalist College, was offered at a satellite campus on the Deleware-Munsee First Nation Reserve. Every six weeks, Clarence went to the campus for an intensive one-week session. For two years, a friend would drive him to the reserve, and Clarence stayed in a motel for the week. Often his sister picked him up at the end of the week. Post-secondary education was a new world for Clarence.

> It was one thing to get your grade 12, but then being enrolled in college, that was a whole different sense of accountability.

To add to the challenges, he was also learning about some intimidating subjects, such as traditional medicines. "At the time, I still had an uneasiness around the medicines," he says.

> I didn't feel good enough. Some people were brought up in the culture and given teachings since they were infants. I was never brought up in that culture. I was never exposed to that. My identity was missing. It's funny because when I was growing up as a foster child, the identity was missing. And then as an adult when I was reconnecting with my culture, the identity was also missing there.

Despite being outside his comfort zone, he started feeling comfortable enough to participate in class. Soon, he was thriving in the program.

> It was a whole different approach to learning: We learned in a circle. We did the medicines. We worked with papers. There was no pressure. They accepted me for who I was, and they let me take as much time as I needed to feel comfortable and confident — speaking from my heart, sharing from my heart.

In July 2013, about a year into the AEI program, Clarence found full-time work at House of Friendship as a Shelter-to-

Housing Stability Case Worker. While the new job was exciting, it was also daunting.

> The job was working with men who were at risk of homelessness. I would work with ten high-acute men who had a range of one or more challenges — either developmental, mental health, addiction, or mobility. And I would say every one of these men suffered trauma in one way or another in their lives. It was my role to find them housing and to keep them housed to the best of my ability.

The job was exactly the kind of work Clarence was hoping for, but it was also a challenging experience.

> There were a lot of assumptions going through my mind about how the men would react to me being there working with them as a support worker. Because it wasn't that long ago that I was living on a different side of the fence. So there was a level of anxiety, a certain element of fear. But I wasn't there to impress anybody. I was just there as a helper.

Clarence thrived in the position and quickly earned the men's respect and trust. His team of co-workers and leaders also supported him as he learned the job.

> They were there to let me do what I needed to do to find my footing as a helper in this community. And that was refreshing, looking back.

His management also encouraged him in his studies and accommodated his class schedule. When he was at AEI, Clarence had a great deal to learn.

> That's where I picked up a lot of my teachings about how to act, how to live, how to be grateful, how to acknowledge, how to approach, how to thank. I made a Grandmother Drum there. That was the first time that I made a drum, and I birthed it. We called the spirit into that drum. Before that, yes, I had sacred objects, but they really didn't have a place. After that, I started collecting things and building the bundle for the community that I live in. I was able to have a stronger voice about the responsibilities that I had with building and carrying the bundle. In college they encouraged us to start building bundles.

Clarence started using his bundle for speaking engagements. In Circle, he would share his life story together with the teachings he had learned on the way. "I carry it for the community," he explains.

Clarence speaking at Kitchener Public Library

Clarence received a holistic assessment from his AEI instructors, which involved a private meeting with an instructor and Elder in which they reviewed the wellness of his mind, body, spirit, and emotions. They shared a vision in which they saw Clarence sitting in a canoe tied to the shore and they encouraged him to untie the canoe and allow himself to be swept away in the river of life.

> And that river of life is scary, especially when you have to learn how to navigate all alone. But it can also be beautiful.

Clarence prepared to give himself over to that river of life when he graduated on July 4, 2014. He now had a connection to something that would ground him in his work and life — people who would help him learn about Indigenous culture and walk the path of a helper.

> Getting that diploma was one of the best things in my life. There was a different level of commitment and accountability. I also have to remember that there was a lot of people who helped me get there and complete that diploma.

After graduating, Clarence continued to work at House of Friendship.

> It was frontline work. It was demanding. But it was a time in my life where I was able to see a certain softness in these men who are always seen but seldom heard.
>
> They say usually after two years when you're doing that kind of work people burn out. I was lucky. I had good boundaries. I had good self-care at the time. And I have a really good support network where I can call people up, talk to them. I can share

what I'm struggling with, and they can give me perspectives. They can give me options. They can give me challenges.

Clarence continued to work as a case worker at House of Friendship for three and a half years.

HAVING BEEN fortunate to find an apartment that was subsidized by Supportive Housing of Waterloo (SHOW), he realized that most individuals graduating from treatment cannot find affordable and safe living arrangements.

> When I came out of treatment, I noticed there was a gap in the system. There was no place for men to come and live that was clean and safe after completing treatment. I was lucky because I had SHOW, but a lot of people weren't so lucky.

Soon after he had started volunteering at St John's Kitchen, Clarence had a meeting with Jennifer and told her about a vision he had for the community: safe and affordable living arrangements for people coming out of treatment for addiction. She said that he was absolutely correct but there was no funding for it.

> After she confirmed with me that I was onto something, I was like a dog with a bone. I've heard that about me so many times in my life.

Clarence started talking with some of his connections. He started collecting letters of support from professionals in the community.

> I went to nurses. I went to doctors. I went to bail officers. I went to councillors, and I managed to get nine

letters of support from community members who agreed that there's a need for this type of housing in our community.

Those conversations ignited a flame. I can say that flame almost went out a few times, but little did I know that there were more and more conversations being had about the need for post-treatment housing.

Two years later, in 2014, three organizations — The Working Centre, House of Friendship, and Stirling Mennonite Church — combined efforts to open a dry house for individuals who have graduated from addictions treatment. Stirling Mennonite Church owned and maintained the houses, The Working Centre took the lead on operations, and House of Friendship played a supportive role. Clarence was a key player for figuring out logistics to get the houses up and running, and then he took on a role as a volunteer support worker.

> I was paired up with a man staying in the house. I would meet with him once a week. I would make sure that he's actively working on his recovery. I would help him navigate our community and assess his progress. I was not a counsellor. I was not a sponsor. I was a support worker. I was offering him support.

Seeing that dry house become a reality was a huge source of encouragement for Clarence.

> That was my first vision. Hard work and determination and talking to other individuals who had the same passion made it all possible.

Clarence was quickly becoming embedded in the social service sector of the region. He was being asked to join boards of non-profit organizations. He was invited to more and more speaking engagements. He was hosting healing circles for men in the community. He felt good about the work he was doing. But through the excitement he had a nagging uncertainty.

> My circumstance was: I've been visiting the Region of Waterloo for fifty-two years and I feel a stronger sense of belonging there than I do to my traditional territory of the Chapleau Cree First Nation peoples. But that also ties into the residential schools, CAS and the foster care system. Because of those destructive systems that were put in place by the government, I never had a chance to have the experience of growing up on my traditional territory.

In the summer of 2014, Clarence decided to take a few weeks off to visit Fox Lake Reserve. He wanted to visit with family, and he felt that he needed to figure out where he truly belonged. He boarded a Greyhound bus in August for the long trip north.

16

FOX LAKE RESERVE

I n 1982, descendants of the Chapleau Cree met in Sault Ste
Marie to discuss reactivating their First Nation. An environ-
mental study found the old reserve uninhabitable due to land
contamination. As a result, in 1989, representatives of the Chapleau Cree negotiated with the federal and provincial governments
and the Chapleau municipality for a new reserve location. After a
successful negotiation, Fox Lake Reserve was established approximately five kilometres southwest of the town of Chapleau. It was
roughly two thousand five hundred acres — a significant increase
from the original reserve's 160 acres — and its southern border sat
on the Nebskwashi River.

Since Fox Lake Reserve was established, many Chapleau Cree
members have returned to their Nation, including some of
Clarence's family. Abby took Clarence to visit his family in the
early '90s, just as the First Nation was beginning to reorganize.
Clarence remembers that there were only a couple houses on the
land back then. Now it contains over thirty homes, a senior's residence, administrative and ceremonial buildings, and a band-owned
gas bar. Chapleau Cree First Nation is rebuilding.

By the time the bus reached the city of Guelph, only 20 minutes after leaving Kitchener, Clarence was already busy writing in his laptop about his thoughts concerning the journey to the Fox Lake Reserve, Chapleau Cree First Nation. He had done a fair amount of journaling during his time in treatment centres, trying to describe all that was going on inside of him, an inner life that had been hidden in long-forgotten places. Now he had a lot to think about, a lot to process. This was the first time he had taken a vacation since he and Stephanie had divorced twelve years prior.

Somewhat unsure about slowing his daily pace, Clarence was hesitant to think of it this time as a vacation. Boredom makes space for unwanted thoughts and yearnings that could lead a person to give up their new life and return to complacency, to the numbed forgetfulness and companionship of the street. He now admits that staying occupied had been a kind of distraction. At one point the previous year, he had been working four part-time jobs at the same time and attending college.

After a short stop in Guelph, the bus drove down to Highway 401 and headed eastbound toward Toronto. Soon they passed beside a smaller suburban city called Milton. On the outskirts of Milton, visible from the highway, there is a giant institution enclosed by a tall, barbed-wire fence: Maplehurst Correctional Complex. With a capacity for up to one thousand five hundred inmates, this is one of Canada's largest prisons.

Almost exactly four years ago, Clarence had been incarcerated at Maplehurst, doing time for an assault charge. It was a relatively short stay — roughly three months — and while it wasn't Clarence's first time in prison, he had been very relieved to get out. When the Greyhound bus rushed by, he wrote:

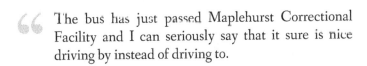

> The bus has just passed Maplehurst Correctional Facility and I can seriously say that it sure is nice driving by instead of driving to.

Soon Toronto was in sight, with its ubiquitous needle-tower

skyline butted up against the expansive Lake Ontario. For Clarence, the city evoked a spectrum of memories. He remembered when he was a young boy that he visited the big city with the Reiers. He remembered the food he ate when they dined out at a Chinese restaurant — it must have been for a special occasion because he had to wear a tie. He remembered eating a hotdog from a street vendor, purchased for him to calm his car-sick stomach. He also had memories of visiting Toronto for school field trips to the Royal Ontario Museum, the CN Tower, and Ontario Place. And of course, painfully, he remembered a traumatic visit from his teenage years of sleeping on the street, overdosing, staying in shelters, interviewing with the local news, and being sexually abused.

The bus arrived in downtown Toronto. Disembarking, Clarence smelled that distinct city odour of diesel emissions and pigeon feces. He stretched his legs and grabbed a bite to eat from a sandwich shop. Walking back through the old terminal, he noticed the place he had slept one night in 1982. He was surprised that he hadn't been kicked out back then. Maybe the security guards took pity on him.

When he re-boarded the bus at noon, Clarence offered the window seat to his neighbour. The gesture was only half-kind because the person sitting behind that seat was constantly kicking it. Over the crackling intercom, the bus driver announced that the expected arrival time for Sudbury would be 6:00 p.m. From there, it was another six hours to Sault Ste Marie, and then four more to Fox Lake Reserve. Clarence settled into his seat. He still had a long journey ahead of him.

After the bus made it to the western shore of Georgian Bay, it began to twist through gorges in the rocky Canadian shield, blasted away when the highway was constructed. This is far enough north that most of the trees Clarence saw through the window were evergreens.

At 4:30 p.m., the bus stopped at a service station in Parry Sound for a short break. After stretching his legs and taking a few breaths of fresh air, Clarence sat and wrote:

> It has been almost eight hours since I started my journey home to Fox Lake, and I can truly say that I'm getting kind of excited.

Eventually, the bus lurched onward, and Clarence watched the scenery pass by — pine trees, cliffs, lakes, more trees.

Sixteen hours after leaving Kitchener, 12:30 a.m., on a Saturday, Clarence's bus arrived at Sault Ste Marie, a small city on the north shore of Lake Superior. His cousin Mike lived there and was waiting for him at the bus depot. After the long ride, with a sore neck and a sore ass, Clarence wrote, "I was never so happy to see a family relation." After a short drive, they pulled up to a suburban home and Mike showed Clarence to his bed. His body hit the guest mattress like a sack of potatoes.

Only a few weeks before this visit north, Clarence had graduated from AEI with a diploma as a Social Service Worker with Indigenous knowledge. He recalls:

> That program slowly brought a circle of understanding, compassion, and acceptance around me. But I was still holding shame of not knowing who I was as a Mushkegowuk man.

While reconnecting with family members and friends, Clarence wanted to work through his dilemma of figuring out where he belonged. But he didn't know how it would be possible to reconnect with a culture and lands that had been deliberately taken from him and his ancestors. He needed to decide if he should move back to his traditional territory or keep living in the city, following the spiritual teachings of his Indigenous mentors there.

"Did you have a good sleep?" Mike asked Clarence as he emerged into the kitchen in the morning. Clarence had not had a good sleep, overtired as he was and in an unfamiliar bed, but he was still happy to be with family. It helped that Mike had already made a pot of coffee. Within the hour they were on the road heading north to Fox Lake Reserve. "On the way to the reserve, Mike and I were catching up on some family, community, and personal views," Clarence explains. The conversation drifted to the negative aspects of the community, the legacies of residential school and stolen land, and Clarence suggested that they try to balance their observations with something positive. "After some reflection we both were able to contribute some positive input."

They arrived at Fox Lake Reserve at 11:30 on a Saturday morning. Clarence had planned his trip to coincide with an annual traditional gathering at the reserve. He would spend two weeks visiting his extended family. When they arrived, lunch was being served at the band office as part of an event in acknowledgement of the children who died at St John's Residential School — the same school that Clarence's grandmother had gone to many years before. After that, they made their way to the new community space on the reserve, a large outdoor arbor, recently constructed for traditional gatherings. Drumming, singing, and dancing was already in full swing for the weekend gathering.

> It was really great to see family and the dancers and drummers, and to feel the connection to ceremony. The day was overcast with periods of slight rain and mist. It was so refreshing to hear the drum, which was like the heartbeat of Mother Earth, and then I knew that I was finally home.

Clarence especially enjoyed a women's singing group who was visiting from Timmins. Their powerful voices sent shivers down his neck. He watched one of his nephews dance in traditional regalia, feeling inspired to witness the next generation so enthusiastic and connected to their Cree heritage.

Throughout the day, his cousin Mike kept him company. Clarence reflects on their relationship:

> From the first time that Mike and I met there was always a connection that I have never felt before and I'm proud to have him as a cousin.

That evening, the two went fishing at a nearby lake. The temperature dropped with a north wind coming off the lake that cut to the bone. They didn't catch anything, but Clarence still savoured the experience. Afterwards, they had dinner with more family. Clarence could hardly engage in the conversations, exhausted as he was from the day's events and lack of sleep the previous night.

The next morning, he was up early again, this time to go fishing with his uncle Michael Cachagee and his cousin Mike. They loaded a pick-up truck and drove to Racine Lake. The gravel road was lined with a thick coniferous forest — pines, cedars, and the odd tamarack every now and then. During the drive, Clarence's uncle reflected on his time in the residential schools, stating simply, "My childhood was ripped away from me."

Clarence was struck by the awful abuses his family and ancestors endured, grateful that he narrowly avoided going to the schools himself.

Abby Cachagee (1991)

But getting back to the beginning. The school didn't leave with you any information. It left a lot of pain. It left a lot of hurt, a lot of confusion. And it scarred you. It didn't tell you how to deal with anything. The only time they said to deal with it was that you had to pray. Everything you had to deal with you had to pray for. It was always me, me, me, pray for me. You weren't given the necessary tools for life. They didn't tell you what life was about.

Today the old people tell us the information that goes back thousands of years. And the Seven Fires, the time now we'll bring back our medicines. We'll bring back our Pipes. The last medicine bundle that came back was over a hundred years old. And in the medicine bundle is the information. So as I said before, I don't know why the Indian schools were built. They were wrong. They served no purpose. They destroyed. They destroyed. They destroyed the family in the same way that the treaties and the Indian Act have destroyed us as a people. One treaty would say something for this group. Another treaty would say something for that group. There was no uniformity across Turtle Island on treaties. Our land claim issues today are dividing us even more.

So that's basically all that the schools have given us, was nothing. They didn't give us nothing. They gave us basically a survival instinct. But that was always with us. They taught us how to lie. They taught us how to steal too. They taught us many [indiscernible]. And yet the people who founded these schools seem to be proud of doing that.

On the shore of Racine Lake, Clarence and the two Mikes (uncle and cousin) transferred fishing supplies into a pontoon boat. Breaks in the clouds hinted at a sunny day to come, much drier than yesterday. There's a family story connected to this lake that involves Clarence's grandfather, Howard Cachagee. It goes something like this.

One day, Howard was out fishing on the lake. Suddenly, a game warden appeared on the far side of the lake, intending to fine Howard for not having a permit to fish on his traditional territory. Well, Howard wasn't having any of it this time, so as soon as he saw the officer launch his boat into the water, he made for the other side of a nearby peninsula. After pulling his canoe onto the shore and flipping it upside down, he ran into the bush. But he only ran so far. Retracing his steps, he walked backwards down to the shore and carefully slid underneath his canoe. He listened as the officer's boat came aground and heard him follow his footsteps into the bush. Moments later, Howard emerged, carefully slid his canoe into the water, and quietly paddled away.

Clarence's fishing trip hit a snag when the boat's engine failed to start. They paddled the boat back to shore and resolved to try again another time.

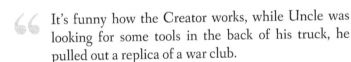

> It's funny how the Creator works, while Uncle was looking for some tools in the back of his truck, he pulled out a replica of a war club.

"Do you want to get rid of it?" Clarence asked.

"Yes, to you! It's yours," uncle Mike replied.

Clarence felt so honoured receiving the gift. He had been hoping over the past couple of years to find one for his bundle. With fishing put on hold, the three family members returned to the reserve and joined in the ongoing ceremonies. The sun was fully shining. As Clarence watched his nephew dance once again, he noticed a small pendant on his regalia and recognized it as an object that was gifted to all the Survivors of Shingwauk Indian Residential School. His own father had passed one just like it down to him, but during Clarence's years of transient homelessness and addiction, he had lost the pendant. Clarence journaled:

> The ceremony filled me with a sense of belonging and connectedness.

After the end of the ceremony, there was a community feast, and Clarence had a chance to speak with the Nation's Chief who encouraged him to continue to share his story, especially with others who are Indigenous. When he got home that night, his aunt told him she had a special gift for him. It was a copy of his father's pendant that he had lost all those years ago. Was it a coincidence or an answered prayer?

The next morning, Clarence woke up to find a thick fog blanketing the land. By noon, the sun had dried away the moisture, and one of Clarence's uncles came to fetch him for fishing. This time Clarence was taken to a more secret fishing spot. No roads lead to this small lake; they had to use ATVs to find it. Once they arrived, Clarence put down some tobacco as an offering to the lake and the fish. The act is from a Cree teaching to always give something back before taking from Mother Earth.

> By the time we arrived, it was 2 p.m., and the sun was shining on my face and the breeze blowing on my back. Uncle was the first to get a fish and it was a walleye; within minutes I caught one, also a walleye. The game was on for almost four straight hours; we were catching fish one right after the other.

By Tuesday, Clarence was finally sleeping soundly through the night. He journaled:

I woke up today to the sound of rain and the tranquility of the North.

Over the next several days, he went on many more fishing trips with his uncles and cousins. And he caught a lot of fish. Some of his cousins taught him how to clean the different species.

One day on the way to Racine Lake — after the boat motor had been replaced — Clarence asked his uncle about his family's history. Uncle Mike shared stories about the brutality he had witnessed in the residential schools. He explained that the schools were in many ways akin to manual labour camps because each day the children worked in the fields or in the wood-shop. He also talked about their family's Cree heritage, saying that their traditional territory is not close to Moose Factory, as Clarence had presumed. They were descendants of Inland Cree, which is why their reserve lands are so far south, compared to where most Cree live, closer to the James and Hudson Bays.

Reflecting on the impact of colonization, Clarence told his uncle that he still struggles with love and affection. He told Mike,

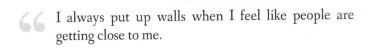 I always put up walls when I feel like people are getting close to me.

Mike let Clarence know that is how their family coped in the schools. They showed no emotions. They put up walls. They disconnected and shielded themselves from anyone and everyone, friendly and unfriendly.

Clarence understood that many of his own struggles and challenges had been transferred across generations into his own life. Like his father and mother, he struggles with addiction. Like his grandfathers and grandmothers, he is afraid of being abandoned.

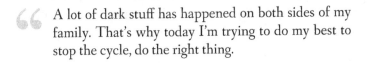 A lot of dark stuff has happened on both sides of my family. That's why today I'm trying to do my best to stop the cycle, do the right thing.

In the back of Clarence's mind was his desire to be a helper, and he wanted to get some guidance from his cousin Johnny Saylors, who is recognized as an Elder in the community. Johnny was living at the seniors home on the reserve and Clarence visited him one day, gifting him a Tobacco Tie and asking for guidance.

"You just keep doing what you're doing," Johnny said. "Helpers don't pick sides or make enemies. We are equals."

A few days later, Johnny invited Clarence for lunch in town.

> On the way to Chapleau, Johnny started asking me if I had a bundle and what was in it. Then in a round-about way he said that he had something to give me if I was ready for the responsibility. He said he had two, and since I had been up here, he had been wondering if he should offer it to add to my bundle.

Eventually Johnny showed Clarence what he had in mind: it was a very sacred object. "It was a rite of passage, a responsibility," says Clarence.

> To carry this sacred object for the people, for healing, is an honour. This object was specifically for the men, and it was meant to be brought back to the community.

After two weeks of staying on the reserve with various family members, Clarence wrote in his journal as he prepared to leave:

> I feel blessed to have all these wonderful people that I can call family. The weather today is overcast, cool, with a slight breeze from the west. I have packed, stripped the bed, washed the sheets, and swept the floor. The feelings are already starting, and I will struggle saying goodbye.

His aunt drove him to Sault Ste Marie, where he met up with cousin Mike who was driving to Toronto and had offered to take Clarence back to Kitchener. At the end of his visit, the question of where to live still bothered Clarence.

> I wanted to live in a community where people have similar values to mine, where we walk with and support people living on the fringe. And where we're doing it as equals.

Much like his ancestors had before him, after travelling nine hundred kilometres north to reacquaint with family, celebrate culture, and exchange gifts, he went south again, back to the land on which he was born, the Grand River Valley. Sitting in the car with his cousin, Johnny's gift carefully packed in his bag, Clarence thought about his community in Kitchener-Waterloo:

> This community tolerated me at my worst times, but this community also embraced me when I was willing to come back as a new person with new values, with new purpose, and new direction and meaning.
>
> I want to be around a community that is there for the people, and I think Kitchener-Waterloo is that community, for me anyways. I feel connected. I have a belonging here. I have history. And I feel like this community has been here for me, through the very early stages of my life, through the middle stages — they've watched and, I guess, cared for me when I couldn't watch and care for myself — and then for them to accept me and welcome me back when I was ready to be on a different road: it's a pretty honourable thing, for me anyways.

It's like an Eagle Feather. It's always thicker at the bottom and then the stem gets smaller and thinner. That represents the stages of life. When you're young, you need a bigger base to stand on, but as you get older, that quill or that stem of the Eagle Feather gets smaller and smaller and smaller. And even when I was forty-five years old, it was like I had to relearn everything all over again, because I believe — and there's documentation out there — when you start using drugs, you stop growing, you stop maturing, you stop developing. So, as a forty-five-year-old man, I had to relearn everything all over again — how to think, how to feel, how to speak, how to act, how to process.

I know that life is a healing journey and I'm on this journey for the rest of my life. And I'm okay with that.

A few months later, on his way to work a shift as a housing outreach worker, Clarence took a coincidental bus ride. When he boarded, he saw an old friend in one of the seats who waved him over. They started to catch up on life, and Clarence started to tell him his story, how he got into the work he was doing at the time.

While they were chatting, a woman, without considering them, took the seat in front of the two. That woman was Margaret Reier, Clarence's foster sister. Neither of them had spoken or seen each other for over twenty years. Margaret overheard the conversation between the two men behind her and it piqued her interest. After a while she recognized the voice of the man who spoke. Margaret recalls the incident: "It was surreal. Because, first of all, I was just listening to kind of an interesting conversation between two people. He was talking about his job. He was working for House of Friendship, and I already knew that he did because I'd read about it in an article. But I didn't approach him at that time."

Ken Reier, Clarence's foster father, had recently passed away. Clarence had heard about his passing but was too nervous to attend the funeral. Margaret admits that she was bitter about the fact that Clarence hadn't surfaced for the funeral, not even a telephone call. She knew that if she tried to speak with him during the bus ride, she would only have had pointed questions to ask. Still, here he was, in the flesh, clearly on a new path, living a new life. When the bus reached Charles Street terminal, Margaret chanced a glance at Clarence as they disembarked. Sure enough, it was him. Later that week Margaret explained the chance encounter to her mother, Eileen, who was disappointed that Margaret hadn't said anything. Margaret figured that it was likely she would see him again since they apparently shared the same bus route — "I thought I'd see him again on the bus, but I never did."

Still, the coincidence piqued her curiosity and Margaret later searched for Clarence online through LinkedIn. Sure enough, she found his profile and saw that he was active in the downtown Kitchener community. She wanted to reach out but wondered how to frame it in a positive manner. She began to draft an email.

At the same time, Clarence received a notification that Margaret had viewed his profile. Nervous about reconnecting with the Reiers after all these years, Clarence sent a short message to Margaret, leaving the ball in her court.

> I must say this is quite the surprise. Lots has changed in my life over the years, I have thought of you time to time, and I hope that you're doing well.

Margaret got the notification just as she was drafting an email to Clarence and that confirmed it for her. She sent the email. Clarence read it and responded.

> I sent Margaret a lengthy reply explaining what happened to me in the last twenty years. Right at the end I said, 'Today I'm a helper and I like to think that

that was due to the Reiers' helping me when I needed it the most.'

Margaret asked Clarence if he could find it in his heart to contact his mother, Eileen, who was currently living in a seniors' residence in Waterloo. Within the week Clarence called Eileen and arranged a meeting with her.

> It was a mind-blowing experience. I can remember when I walked in there — I think it was dinner time and she was eating — I ran into one of the workers who said that Eileen was having supper and that she'd be done in fifteen or twenty minutes. So I sat there in the lounge for a minute. Then I asked the worker to point Eileen out again, and I went over to talk with her. And it blew me away. I was taken aback by how old she looked. Then when she was done eating, I wheeled her back to her room in her wheelchair. That's when we reconnected. All the stories came out. I can remember I started crying, because maybe there was some shame there, maybe some remorse. But then also maybe tears of joy. I gave her a red-tailed Hawk Feather, which represents strength, guardianship, and far-sightedness.

> It was a time of accountability because I had to have some hard conversations. It was also a time of sorrow because I had to have a conversation with my mom about how Ken passed.

> It was also a time when you had to have those hard conversations bringing up the past. She had to fill me in about what happened in the last 15-20 years, in regards to relationships, deaths, and life in general.

Margaret commented on the meeting: "It was really good for her soul. She put out a lot of love raising him; it was really good to get that back."

After Clarence and Eileen met, Clarence said that he would like to get the whole family together — Eileen, his foster siblings, and their spouses. Eileen agreed and soon a date was set.

CLARENCE ARRIVED AT THE SENIORS' residence in Waterloo at noon on Saturday, December 5, 2015. At the far end of the dining hall there was a small, enclosed dining room which was reserved for the meeting. Staff were preparing to serve Clarence and his foster family a light lunch. He walked through the hall past a small crowd gathered to watch a singer at the front who was entertaining the guests with Christmas carols. The singer was a solo act, playing an electric keyboard and singing into a mic with a small amp on the ground. The dining room had a large window that overlooked the dining hall, so the family gathered inside could see the crowd gathered outside for the festivities. The crowd could see Clarence and his family too, but everyone was mostly preoccupied with the holiday entertainment.

Members of Clarence's foster family were already there when Clarence arrived. It was quiet when he walked into the room. He hugged Eileen first, then moved around the room in a circle, hugging each of his foster siblings and their partners. There was surprised recognition in their faces.

Clarence had brought his drum with him, and before lunch was served, he asked to sing a song for Eileen. The family agreed and he carefully unpacked his Grandmother Drum from a leather sack, hoisting it up. He closed his eyes and began to sing in a clear, strong voice. Some of the crowd outside peered into the dining room, curious about the man with a hide-drum singing a different song. As Clarence sang, his family listened, tears welling up in their eyes. Eileen's eyes were closed.

I opened the gathering in song. I sang the Strong
Woman Song for mom.

I shared my story.

EPILOGUE BY CLARENCE

When I went back and met with the Reiers, it really wasn't all about me at that time. I did that because I wanted the Reiers — the family that took in me and my sibling — to have a really good understanding of what I went through. Because I didn't talk about a lot in the past. They could only assume why I did what I did. So I wanted to disclose my whole life. And it's unfortunate that my oldest brother didn't come. All the other siblings came but he chose not to come because he doesn't consider me his brother or sibling. And that's okay. The other siblings and my mom, they got to hear my story. I needed to do that for myself and I needed to do that for them, so that they would have an understanding of what I struggled with my whole life. It was a very emotional time. I needed to do that for closure. And I needed to do that for my mom. I needed to show her the utmost respect that I could give at that time. And that was to be totally vulnerable and that was to totally tell the truth about everything that I experienced in my whole life.

I wanted to make those amends before she made her journey. I feel honoured that I was able to do that.

When you hear that Hand Drum, let it connect you. Let that drum connect you to your ancestors. Let that drum connect you to the spirits. Let that drum connect you to the Creator. Because when we drum and when we sing, that's a form of prayer.

I never wanted to sing in front of people. I never thought I'd sing in front of people. I thought people would make fun of me. Even today when I see traditional people and full-blooded people, when I sing in front of them, I get nervous. But I do my best. I close my eyes and I sing. And it's an honour to sing for the people and for Creation.

I want people to know that regardless of how hard your life has been, or how broken you are, that you're not alone. I want people to know that there's something out there that will help you. I want them to know that the blood of their ancestors still runs through their veins and if it weren't for their ancestors they wouldn't be here today. I want them to know that they're all sacred. They're all loved. They're all worthy. I want them to know that they can all be part of something. They can be united. I want them to know that it's okay to be who you are, whether you're a man, you're a woman, or you're Two-Spirited. There's no judgement. We're all equals and we're all special in our own way, and we're all sacred.

I think connecting with self, with who you really are, is so important. It's looking deep inside your mind, body, spirit, and emotions and knowing what your triggers are, what your fears are, what you struggle with. And then through awareness and support being able to work through those things. One of the hardest things is asking for help and being vulnerable — and not seeing that as a weakness. Life is truly a gift. We are all beautiful. But at times there are things that have power over us, that prevent us from developing, moving forward, and finding out who we truly are and what our roles are. I believe we all have certain roles and certain gifts and those gifts are meant to be shared. The gifts that I have are to bring change and to bring people together.

The north wind brings change. Everyone in Creation has gifts. Sometimes people know what those gifts are and sometimes people have no idea. It takes time and patience but also willingness and courage to find out what your gifts are and to start using them.

I got caught in a cycle of homelessness for eight years. But while I was in that cycle, I knew that I had responsibilities. I knew that I had responsibilities not only to myself but to my daughters and to Creation. Plus I didn't want to die. Addictions to alcohol and drugs can be a slow suicide. When I was homeless and when I was caught hard in the grips of addiction, I left all those responsibilities that I had. I just didn't care. But something just kept coming to me, saying 'Clarence, this is the end of your life; this is the end of your road. If you keep doing what you're doing, you're going to see that Western Door pretty soon. Or you can put the plug in the jug, put the dope down, and go do what you need to do to become a helper and then come back and help the people.'

I think I always had it deep inside of me — that gratitude for people who helped me. I wanted to give it back to Creation. I wanted to give it back in some way, somehow, because I was so grateful for those different people in my life that invested their time in me. I figured, 'Hey, I want to be a helper, I have the experience, I have the resume, I have the degree in homelessness. Right? I have a degree in trauma. Right? I have many degrees.'

But I couldn't have done it without help. There were so many people who helped me along the way starting with my parents Ken and Eileen, because they really helped me, they taught me how to live. That family that I stayed with, that we stayed with, they helped me. And that's why they say that the first word that ever came out of my mouth was 'teacher'. It wasn't 'mom'; it wasn't 'dad'. It was teacher because Eileen and Ken were teaching me how to be a boy and how to live.

So then when I sobered up, there were many people who helped me, many that we have mentioned in this book. But there are so many others that we didn't mention like: Hilton King, Kathy Absolon, Myeengun Henry, Dr Max Solace, Mike Brown, Mary Anne Spencer, Heather Green, Slam, and the list just goes on and on and on. Because I finally found my pathway back to culture. But it was hard. It was awkward. It was scary. And the thing was, I was doing it all by myself. I didn't have any helpers to help me take those first steps back to culture; I had decide to do that on my own. But once I made that connection through The Healing of the Seven Generations then things started to align. And that was hard because I wasn't brought up in that culture. I remember Donna saying — and Donna and I are good friends today — but she says — she always smiles when she remembers the first time that she saw me — but then she shakes her head because she says, "Clarence, you were dirty. You had two black eyes. But you still found the strength to come in here and talk to me." She says, "I wish I would have taken a picture to compare then and now."

I believe that you can't really know where to go unless you know where you came from. I couldn't truly learn who I was as a child because of the Sixties Scoop, so I had to relearn it as an adult. Connecting with my Indigenous identity gave me a pathway to healing.

There was a gentleman who I met recently. His name was Dean Peachey. He said, 'Clarence I'm going to tell you a story about Ken Reier.' He says — and this Dean has caught me off guard a couple times — he says that there was a time when 'in Mannheim Church when there were all these little kids running around. And you know Mannheim: they're Mennonite people; they're kind of reserved. So somebody was going to stop these children from running because they were making noise in the church — they were being kids.' Dean said that my dad Ken — and Ken never said anything; he was a big strong German guy, a man of very few words — but at that time Ken said, 'Don't stop them from being children. Let them be children. Let them use their voice. Because when I was young, somebody told me to be quiet and I never got my voice back.' And that story just blew me away; it was so emotional hearing him tell me what Ken said all those years ago.

When I reflect back, there were so many people in my life that watched over me; and when I reconnected with my culture, I was taught that the Creator always watched over me, and my Ancestors were always with me, and my Spirit Helpers were always there. When we discuss far-sightedness, that's where the visionary comes in, for me anyways. I believe that I was given this life by the Creator and all that the

Creator wants back in return is for me to instil change, big or small, in myself, in my community, and in Creation.

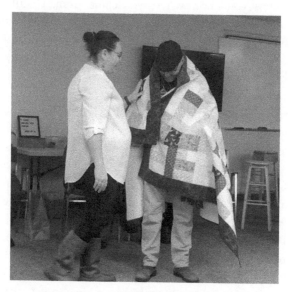

Clarence receives a "Quilt for Survivors" from Vanessa Genier and gifts her an Eagle Feather

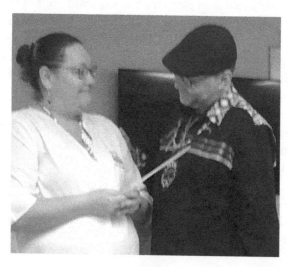

A CONVERSATION WITH CLARENCE

The proceeds of this book are going toward a vision you have for this community. What have you got in mind?

I knew that if I wanted to be a helper first I had to help myself. I had to invest time in myself. I had to get away from everybody and everything. And then I went away to One-Seventy-Four King and I went to Native Horizons and Kiikeewanniikaan. Then I got a diploma at AEI. And then I started working in the community as a helper and I noticed there was a gap, not only to land but to culture. There wasn't enough land-based resources available to community members. And the only opportunities that were available, they had to travel hours and hours outside of our community to find that.

I started talking to some people and we found a pathway out to a retreat centre near Guelph. We were there for a couple years and I was able to pilot some land-based teachings. And then I started talking to my supports and I said how can we bring the Lodge back to Waterloo Region. That's when I met the Pfennings. And true allyship is happening today right in front of us. The Pfennings have property and they wanted to form a relationship to Indigenous communities to allow access to the land for cultural and ceremonial purposes. We can talk about reconciliation but that's a long way away. We still have five more generations to get there. So let's talk about allyship. That's more attainable. That's happening right now. Indigenous people need more space, we need more land, and the Pfennings stepped up.

That's where we started Crow Shield Lodge. My experiences showed me that the community I serve needed a Healing Lodge that is guided by an Indigenous lens and a holistic approach to healing and learning. This vision of a Healing Lodge came from my own personal experience of being in one and reaping the benefits. It gave me a starting point and a new beginning. Crow Shield Lodge sits on four pillars, which are healing, education, land stewardship, and reconciliation. It is run by the spirit. We don't push anything here. We let the spirit guide us. We let the spirit direct us. All of our facilitators are Indigenous. All of our Fire Keepers are Indigenous. We train and we invest in the next generations.

It's an amazing place. It gives people something they've never had before. It gives them that belonging. It gives that connectedness. It gives them a place to go. Not only to educate but to unlearn and to heal. I can say that this year we've had 600 people through this site, through this land-based site. We've given people a starting point to help them unlearn and we've also helped over 120 people heal through Sweat Lodge ceremony. Then we noticed that the need for healing is in such high demand that we couldn't serve everyone who wanted healing. So we decided that we need a second site. We've been talking to the Region of Waterloo for almost two years. They were the first people we went to. We invited them on this journey with us. And then they offered us keys to our second site on regional property at the Ken Seiling Museum.

And it just keeps growing and growing and just keeps getting better. And now what we're looking for is a couple more sites because we want to have four sites in this region. One in each corner, one in each doorway. And we want to find some land so that we can bring a Healing Lodge to this region, a Healing Lodge for Indigenous and non-Indigenous people. That's what Crow Shield Lodge is all about. It's about bringing all nations together as equals, so that we can start walking down a new road, a new path of understanding. And we have to start talking about those truths. Because until those truths are acknowledged nothing can ever move forward. People are always saying, "Oh, why don't the Indigenous people just get over it? It wasn't my generation; it wasn't my family. They have enough stuff." Well, we can't get over it because that's our family, those are our ancestors, those are our nations, those are our community members that they're still finding buried in those residential schools. We've always known that those children are there, it's just when we spoke to the government about it, they said there's no evidence. And now there's evidence and now those numbers are up to ten thousand, ten thousand children they're still finding in those schools. That's an example of the truths that we need to talk about. The residential school system has had a horrendous impact on my family. And it's still going. It's still going into the next generation, but I wanted to do my best to stop that, stop that from going into my daughters, stop that from going into my granddaughter.

The time is right and the time is ripe to be doing this kind of work. I want to thank Wilmot Township and Waterloo Region for stepping outside of their comfort zone and walking with us.

In this Lodge, people are transformed. When they come out to this environment, it's different than any board room, or any meeting room. When you're on the earth, when your feet are on the ground, when you're near the fire — fire is community, fire is life, fire is warmth, fire is food. And then when you add the sacred objects and the medicines — it's just the perfect environment for the right experience.

I have a basic understanding that to be broken is to be ordinary, and that everybody is broken in one way or another. Some people will speak about their brokenness. Some people won't — and that's okay. But to have a place that is safe where people can speak about their brokenness and have the opportunity to release it, I think that kind of place would be special, unique, and beneficial to this community and other communities. You have to have a place where you can share your vulnerable truths without judgement.

There is a teaching that when we use substances or drink alcohol, our spirit leaves our body for four days. After four days of sobriety, we are able to pick up the medicines again and rekindle that relationship. Many life experiences can displace our spirit. I can say firsthand that my spirit was displaced for many years, for a majority of my lifetime. When I reconnected with my spirit, I found purpose, meaning, and direction. Crow Shield Lodge is a place where people can reconnect with spirit.

Can you elaborate on the objects in your healing bundle, what it means to carry a bundle, and how those objects relate to various stages of your life?

The bundle that I carry has healing properties for me but it's also a community bundle. There are different kinds of bundles, some are personal, some are sacred, and some are community bundles. The bundle that I bring out is the community bundle. It has sacred objects in it that people can look at, use, and touch. All the objects in the bundle have certain qualities, some are sacred, some are medicine, and some are there for teachings. The bundle represents culture, healing, and purpose, and it keeps me connected to who I am as a helper. I was taught that we all have different goals and different gifts. One of my gifts is to bring people together, to walk with them, and to not judge them. As a helper, I feel like I was gifted a second chance at life; I want to make the most out of it, not only to help myself but to also help others.

During your journey, you absorbed a lot of Indigenous Knowledge from Elders and community members, in Indigenous treatment centres, and at the Anishinabek Education Institute. How have those teachings impacted your social work practice?

That's a very deep question because I remember that, over the years, I've had many helpers. I've had many people support me or work with me. And some of the people I remember the most were the ones that just acted normal: They didn't want anything from me. They held a space for me where it was safe. And they had enough understanding where they didn't probe too much. They would just look at me in the eye and meet me as an equal. I can also remember going to other people and having these people sit across from me, and they'd sit me in their chair, and they'd look at me and they'd cross their legs and they'd go, "Oh really? And how did that make you feel? Can you share a little more about that topic with me?" Come on. Let's just get over that. I want you to work with me and take me deep places.

So I guess that had an impact on how I was going to look at how to be a helper or a good helper, where I could help somebody with their mind, their body, their spirit, and their emotions. It's funny, when I first got into this kind of work, I always said that I got into it because I could relate. I've been there. I know what they've been through. There's nobody better to talk to but somebody who's been there. But after some conversations with some people and some friends, I found out that I do this kind of work because I get something back. I get recognition. I feel important. I feel worthy enough to serve these individuals. Some might say that's selfish but I call it self-full.

Now my life is all about connecting with spirit because the essence of spirit is at the centre of everything. That means that when you're walking with somebody, when you're supporting them, you meet them with your spirit, your spirits connect, and that's when the deep work starts to happen. Those teachings I learned laid a foundation to help me become a holistic helper in this community. The bottom line is that I'm trying to be a part of positive change— within people, places, and things. I'm trying to be a man that walks with strength but then also has humility.

What are some opportunities and challenges that you see for rebuilding relationships between Indigenous and non-Indigenous people here in the Grand River Valley?

The time is ripe for conversations about reconciliation. Reconciliation means becoming accountable to past wrongs. We have to know where we came from in order to know where we are going. But at the same time, I choose not to get stuck in the past. It's okay to look as long as you don't stare — you know what I mean? Sometimes it turns into blame and shame. The question is: will that move anybody forward? I want to work together. To me, it's not about us and them; it's about we. What can we do together? When you talk about spirit, there is no colour. When you talk about healing, there is no colour. When you talk about wellness, there is no colour. When you talk about unity, there is no colour.

We need strong men. We need strong women. We need to bring them to the forefront. We need to acknowledge our Ancestors. We need to take care of our Ancestors. And we need to prepare the next seven generations because we're at a fork in the road. We either go one way where it's all greed. It's ego. It's materialistic things. It's power. It's destruction. It's envy. Or we go down the other fork in the road, where we get back to ceremonies. We get back to feeling united. We get back to living in harmony. We get back to being connected to Creation, to the world.

We are connected to everything. We're connected to the two-legged, to the four-legged, to the winged ones, to the swimmers, to the crawlers. We're connected to the trees. We're connected to all living plants. We're connected to the four winds. We're connected to the rocks, to the minerals, to the mountains. We're connected to the lakes, the rivers, the streams, and the oceans. And all those that I said right there are all of our relations. And we're connected to them as equals within the circle of life. We're connected living on Mother Earth. And we're all connected as one under the eyes of the Creator.

AFTERWORD BY MICHAEL CACHAGEE

I was asked by Clarence Michael if I would be willing to supply an endorsement for his book presently preparing to go to print. My reply was a definite and resounding yes as it would be my pleasure to do. I will explain my reasoning and the motivation to do so.

Clarence is my nephew and the son of my late brother Clarence (Abbie) Cachagee and as such I not only commend his energy and the initiative he took to complete such an important task, but more so the courage to do so. Clarence like so many of the other children of the Indian Residential School Survivors experienced a life of several changes and challenges as a result of his father attending the schools. Calling them "schools" is perhaps a misnomer as those of us who had attended them now consider our time in them as being incarcerated.

Taking this history in today's perspective it has been proved beyond all doubt that what his father had endured as a result of his time in two different Indian Residential Schools — including extreme cases of physical, emotional/psychological and sexual abuse — the impacts and the suffering associated with this experience are passed on down to their intergenerational offspring. In Clarence's case these impacts were devastating, and it resulted in him, and his siblings being raised in a broken home due to the breakdown of his parents' marriage. Later he would end up being a ward of the Ontario Children Aid Society. All of this would lead to serious breakdown in Clarence's ability to cope and deal with emotions and life challenges that are usually grounded in being raised in a loving and caring family environment. After years of substance abuse and personal behavioural challenges, Clarence has overcome the challenges this lifestyle presented him, to become the person he is today.

Clarence had to undertake a life-changing journey and to do so he had to return back to where his identity as a young Cree man was imbedded in — and that was his spiritual identity. Once Clarence began to understand and embrace his Native Spirituality, he moved into a position whereby his emotional and mental challenges became something he could learn to master. Now with the help and assistance from the other self-help programs, which also made an important part of who he was now, he was now ready to live and become part of who the Creator had originally made him and his father to be — and that is strong and clean-living Eellou (Cree) men. I am very proud to have been a part of Clarence's recovery and have watched him as he has transitioned into becoming this new man.

— Michael Cachagee (uncle of Clarence Cachagee)

ACKNOWLEDGMENTS

First of all, we'd like to acknowledge all the people who have walked with us, supported us, and gifted us their time and knowledge. If it weren't for them, we wouldn't be here today.

We are especially thankful for the courage and generosity of Clarence's relatives and foster family who shared their knowledge, time, and gifts with us. That includes, but is not limited to, Michael Cachagee for sharing his knowledge and for providing feedback on chapters that included the history of Mushkegowuk people and Chapleau Cree First Nation; and Marjorie Lee for agreeing to an interview and sharing about her life and brother.

This book wouldn't have been possible without the generosity, honesty, and time granted by all our interviewees. It was an honour to work with all of you. We are also grateful for Algoma University's work interviewing Clarence Hubert Cachagee and sharing with us the archived recording of his truths.

Clarence would like to acknowledge the important people in his life who have helped shape his understanding of Indigenous identity and culture. Some of these people include: Gerard Sagassige, Donna Dubie, Peter Linkletter, Johnny Saylors, Mary Anne Caibaiosai, Hilton King, Kathy Absolon, Myeengun Henry, Peter Schuler, Lois MacDonald, Malcolm Saulis, Grandmother Renee Thomas-Hill, Mary-Ann Spencer, Heather Green, Dorothy French, Harry Snowboy, Lana Brascher, Fran Davis, and Dave Skeen. There are many more that Clarence could name.

Clarence also gives his deepest and most sincere acknowledgement to his partner Nicole Robinson, for her time and patience, her understanding and teaching, and her willingness to walk with him as an equal.

We'd like to express deep gratitude for all our friends and family who supported us financially and emotionally. There are far too many of you to name individually; we felt and continue to feel blessed by a life-giving community of support. And we acknowledge the numerous Mennonite churches that supported us and engaged in dialogue with us during the creation of this book. A big thank you also goes to the Region of Waterloo Arts Fund and the Fretz Publication Fund for providing the financial support that made much of our research, writing, and editing possible.

Karen Kuhnert, Chris Hiller, Dylan Siebert, and Marlene Epp, thank you for taking time to read and provide feedback on an early draft of the introduction and first chapter of the manuscript. We appreciate the support and encouragement from the wonderful folks at *The New Quarterly* (TNQ).

Thank you Jackie Fletcher for taking time to review and provide feedback on writing about Abby's experience in the Residential School System (and writing about the schools). Thank you Kathy Absolon for your careful structural editing of a draft manuscript. And thank you Rhonda Kronyk for your insightful copyediting.

We could not have finished this project without the patient and thoughtful help of our publisher Jonathan Seiling.

We need to acknowledge our ancestors, Indigenous and settler, for their works of love and for the hardships they endured for us to be here today. We also want to acknowledge our connectedness to the sun, to the moon, and beyond. And we acknowledge our connectedness to the two-legged, four-legged, winged ones, swimmers, the four winds, the crawlers, the trees, all plants, the medicines, the rocks, minerals and mountains, and the rivers, streams, and oceans — all as equals within the circle of life. We thank the trees especially for their gift of pulp to make this book possible.

And lastly, thank you, our reader, for joining us on this healing journey.

NOTES

Foreword

1. Used with permission, taken from interview with Clarence Hubert Cachagee, Shingwauk Residential Schools Centre, Algoma University.
2. Eve Tuck, "Suspending Damage: A Letter to Communities," (Harvard Educational Review: September 2009), Vol. 79, No. 3: 416.

Introduction by Clarence

1. Unless another source is referenced, all direct quotations from Clarence Cachagee throughout this book come from interviews with Seth Ratzlaff conducted May 2016 through August 2022, or from an interview conducted by Nathan Stretch, May 27, 2017.

1. Purpose, Meaning and Direction

1. Noble, William C. 2015. "The Neutral Confederacy." The Canadian Encyclopedia. https://www.thecanadianencyclopedia.ca/en/article/neutral.
2. See Susan M. Hill, *The Clay We Are Made Of: Haudenosaunee Land Tenure on the Grand River* (Winnipeg: University of Manitoba Press, 2017).
3. ibid., 87.
4. Leanne Simpson, "Looking after Gdoo-naaganinaa: Precolonial Nishnaabeg Diplomatic and Treaty Relationships," *Wicazo Sa Review* (Fall 2008), 36.
5. Frederick Haldimand. "Haldimand's Proclamation of October 25, 1784." In Johnston, Charles Murray, *The Valley of the Six Nations: A Collection of Documents on the Indian Lands of the Grand River*, 51.

2. Early Years

1. Margaret Reier, interview with Seth Ratzlaff, Kitchener, May 26, 2016.
2. Eileen was also involved in leadership at her church, Mannheim Mennonite. She was the first woman to be elected as an Elder (1981), for which she served six years. See: Ferne Burkhardt, *Full Circles: Mannheim Mennonite Church 1836-1986* (Petersburg, ON: Mannheim Mennonite Church, 1986), 36, 70.
3. Keith Reier, interview with Seth Ratzlaff, Kitchener, June 14, 2016.

4. This quotation from Abby and all subsequent quotations are taken from the interview with Clarence Hubert Cachagee (1991), Shingwauk Residential Schools Centre, Algoma University.

3. Mennonites

1. Sam Steiner, *In Search of Promised Lands* (Herald Press, 2015), 50.
2. Block Number Two was held on lease by Richard Beasley, who soon fell behind in payments to the Six Nations. When Mennonites feared title to the land would be lost, they formed a syndicate — the German Company — to purchase outright two thirds of Block Number Two. The payment was transferred to government trustees who held the funds on behalf of the Six Nations. Most of these funds were squirreled away in offshore accounts in Britain. As of 2022, the Ontario and Canadian governments continue to refuse to provide an accounting for Six Nation's funds that were supposedly managed on their behalf.
3. E. Reginald Good, "Colonizing a People: Mennonite Settlement in Waterloo Township." From *Earth, Water, Air and Fire*, 168.
4. Ibid., 162.
5. Good, "Colonizing a People," 149.
6. Ferne Burkhardt, *Full Circles: Mannheim Mennonite Church 1836-1986* (Mannheim Mennonite Church, 1986), 7.
7. Sam Steiner, *In Search of Promised Lands* (Herald Press, 2015), 148.
8. As related through Eileen's daughter, Margaret Reier, interview with Seth Ratzlaff, Kitchener, May 26, 2016.
9. Johnston, Patrick. *Native Children and the Child Welfare System.* (James Lorimer & Co., 1983), 66-76.
10. Johnston, Patrick. 1981. "Indigenous Children at Risk" *Policy Options*, Nov.-Dec. 1981: 49.
11. Hudson, P. and B. McKenzie, B. (1981, 1985). "Child Welfare and Native People: The Extension of Colonialism." The Social Worker, 49, 63-88.
12. TRC Executive Summary, *Honouring the Truth, Reconciling for the Future*, page 68.
13. TRC volume 5, page 13.
14. TRC volume 5, page 15.
15. https://www.cbc.ca/news/politics/ottawa-settle-60s-scoop-survivors-1.4342462
16. Steiner, *In Search of Promised Lands*, 451.

4. The Western Door

1. Also known by various names such as Mushkegowuk and Eellou/Eeyou in eastern Canada, in western Canada, Cree are also known as Nehiyawak.
2. For much of the content in this chapter, we are indebted to Clarence's uncle, Michael Cachagee, for sharing his knowledge and expertise on the history of

Chapleau Cree First Nation.

3. Victor P. Lytwyn, *Muskekowuck Athinuwick: Original People of the Great Swampy Land* (University of Manitoba Press, 2002), 96.
4. Louis Bird, *Telling Our Stories: Omushkego Legends & Histories from Hudson Bay* (Broadview Press, ltd., 2005), 174.
5. Regina Flannery and M. Elizabeth Chambers, "John M. Cooper's Investigation of James Bay Family Hunting Grounds," *Anthropologica* (28, 1/2, 1986), 127-128.
6. Schreyer, Christine Schreyer, "Travel Routes of the Chapleau Cree: An Ethnological Study." Algonquin Paper-Archive (34), 330.
7. The actual petition for a treaty was written by an HBC trader, Jabez William, who would have had his own economic interests in mind as well. William indicated that the Anishinaabe were desirous of giving up their rights to the land, but historian John S Long argues that what was more likely the case was that the Indigenous hunters desired payments for sharing their land and protection from resource development. See John S Long, *Treaty No. 9*, pg. 40-43.
8. For example, the Ontario government stipulated that no reserve lands contain "any site suitable for the development of water-power exceeding 500 horse-power."
9. Long, "How the Commissioners Explained Treaty Nine," *Ontario History* (Spring 2006) no. 98, 1: 5-6.
10. Long, *Treaty No. 9*
11. Long, *Treaty No. 9*, 333.
12. Duncan C. Scott, et al., *The James Bay Treaty: Treaty Number Nine* (Queen's Printer, 1964).
13. William E McLeod, *The Chapleau Game Preserve: History, Murder, and Other Tales* (Betty Printing, 2004), 6.

5. Disconnecting

1. Children's Aid Society of the Regional Municipality of Waterloo, Record Disclosure for Clarence Cachagee, April 14, 2011.
2. Burtch Correctional Facility closed in 2003 and was eventually demolished. Incidentally, the land on which the facility was located has since been returned to the Six Nations of the Grand River as part of the ongoing Grand River land dispute.

6. New Relationships

1. In our interview, Keith Reier explained that he and his family were confused when they came back to the farm that day, but they guessed at what had happened. Still, Keith acknowledged that his parents had always wished that Clarence had stayed instead of running away.

7. The Schools

1. Roland Chrisjohn, and Sherri Young, Michael Maraun, *The Circle Game: shadows and substance in the Indian residential school experience* (Penticton, BC: Theytus Books Ltd., 2006).
2. The Truth and Reconciliation Commission of Canada, *Honouring the Truth, Reconciling for the Future: Summary of the Final Report of the Truth and Reconciliation Commission of Canada* (Truth and Reconciliation Commission of Canada, 2015), 90-92.
3. RG 10, Vol 6191, File 462-1, part 1. Letter, A. G. Chisholm, Barrister & Solicitor, to Deputy Superintendent General of Indian Affairs, January 14, 1922. Library and Archives Canada. Indian Affairs School Files.

10. Abby's Early Years

1. Clarence Hubert Cachagee, interview at Shingwauk Indian Residential School Centre, Sault Ste Marie, ON, 1991.
2. Quotes from Abby in this chapter are also taken from the interview with Clarence Hubert Cachagee, Shingwauk Residential Schools Centre, Algoma University.
3. Michael Cachagee, interview with Seth Ratzlaff, Fox Lake Reserve, Chapleau Cree First Nation, November 5, 2016.
4. Jean L. Manore, "A Vision of Trust: The Legal, Moral, and Spiritual Foundations of Shingwauk Hall," *Native Studies Review* no. 9, 2 (1993-4), 3.
5. Janet E. Chute, *The Legacy of Shingwaukonse: A Century of Native Leadership* (Toronto: University of Toronto Press, 1998), 43.
6. Jean L. Manore, "A Vision of Trust," 3.
7. Augustine Shingwauk, *Little Pine's Journal: The Appeal of a Christian Chippeway Chief on Behalf of His People* (Toronto: Copp, Clark 1872; facsimile ed. Sault Ste Marie: Shingwauk Project 1991).
8. Carolyn Harrington, "Shingwauk School," *Ontario Indian* (October 1980), 22-26, pg. 26; see also Chute, *The Legacy of Shingwaukonse*.
9. Manore, "A Vision of Trust," 5-6.
10. Harrington, "Shingwauk School," 24.
11. Chute, *The Legacy of Shingwaukonse*, 193.
12. Manore, "A Vision of Trust," 9.
13. Fair Play (pseudonym), "The Future of Our Indians," *The Canadian Indian* (March-June 1891) vol 1 (6-9).
14. Marjorie Lee, interview with Clarence Cachagee and Seth Ratzlaff, Fox Lake Reserve, Chapleau Cree First Nation, November 4, 2016.
15. Cited in, *The Final Report of the Truth and Reconciliation Commission of Canada*, Volume 4, 120.

11. The Cycle

1. Name changed for privacy.
2. Name changed for privacy.

12. Surviving

1. Interview conducted by Seth Ratzlaff with Jennifer Mains, June 14, 2016, Kitchener.
2. Joe and Stephanie Mancini, *Transition to Common Work* (Wilfrid Laurier University Press, 2015), 67.
3. Quoted from: Mancini, *Transition to Common Work,* 81.
4. Interview conducted by Seth Ratzlaff with George Berrigan, February 9, 2016, Kitchener.
5. Donna Dubie, interview with Seth Ratzlaff, Kitchener, August 31, 2016.

13. Out of the Bubble

1. Rick Pengalli, interview with Seth Ratzlaff, Kitchener, June 9, 2016.
2. Name changed for privacy.

14. Reconnecting

1. William Asikinack, 'Sweat-Lodge Ceremony' in https://teaching.usask.ca/indigenoussk/import/sweat-lodge_ceremony.php (accessed October 25, 2022)
2. Anishnawbe Mushkiki Health Access Centre'. n.d. Traditional Teaching: Your Name and Colours: Why Having a Spirit Name is Important', https://mushkiki.com/our-programs/your-name-and-colours/ (accessed Oct 25, 2022)

15. Becoming a Helper

1. Developed by the Kitchener Downtown Community Health Centre's (KDCHC) "Homelessness Advisory Group and partner organizations YWCA, ROOF and Ray of Hope. The award recognizes the unique and important work of peers. It is given to individuals who have been homeless at some time in their life, who are now working to support other people experiencing homelessness in the community." https://kdchc.org/wp-content/uploads/2014/06/KDCHC-Newsletter-Fall-2014.pdf (accessed October 25, 2022)

BIBLIOGRAPHY

Anishnawbe Mushkiki Health Access Centre'. n.d. Traditional Teaching: Your Name and Colours: Why Having a Spirit Name is Important', https://mushkiki.com/our-programs/your-name-and-colours/

Armitage, A. (1995). Comparing the Policy of Aboriginal Assimilation: Australia, Canada, and New Zealand. UBC Press.

Asikinack, William. n.d. 'Sweat-Lodge Ceremony' in https://teaching.usask.-ca/indigenoussk/import/sweat-lodge_ceremony.php

Baker, Patricia. n.d. "Learning...the hard way; Michael Cachagee's reveals scars of residential school experience." Sault Star. http://archives.algomau.-ca/main/sites/default/les/2010-061_007_063.pdf.

Bird, Louis. (2005). Telling Our Stories: Omushkego Legends & Histories from Hudson Bay. PBroadview Press.

Burkhardt, Ferne. (1986). Full Circles: Mannheim Mennonite Church. Published by Mannheim Mennonite Church.

Chisholm, A. G. RG 10, Vol 6191, File 462-1, part 1. Letter to Deputy Superintendent General of Indian Affairs, January 14, 1922. Library and Archives Canada, Indian Affairs School Files.

Chrisjohn, Roland, et al. (2006). The Circle Game: Shadows and substance in the Indian residential school experience. Theytus Books Ltd.

Chute, Janet E. (1998). The Legacy of Shingwaukonse. University of Toronto Press.

Flannery, Regina, and Chambers, M. E. (1986). "John M. Cooper's Investigation of James Bay Family Hunting Grounds." Anthropologica (28, 1/2), 108-144.

Good, E. R. (1998). "Colonizing a People: Mennonite Settlement in Waterloo Township." In Earth, Water, Air and Fire: Studies in Canadian Ethnohistory, edited by David T. McNab. Waterloo: Wilfrid Laurier University Press.

Hanson, Erin. (2009). "Sixties Scoop." First Nations & Indigenous Studies. Accessed February 15, 2018. http://indigenousfoundations.arts.ubc.ca/sixties_scoop/.

Harrington, Carolyn. (1980). "Shingwauk School." Ontario Indian 3, no. 10 (October), 22-26.

Hepworth, P. (1980). "Native Children in Care." In Foster Care and Adoption in Canada. Canadian Council on Social Development. Ottawa.

Hill, Susan M. (2017). The Clay We Are Made Of: Haudenosaunee Land Tenure on the Grand River. Winnipeg: University of Manitoba Press.

Hudson, P. and B. McKenzie, B. (1981, 1985). Child Welfare and Native People: The Extension of Colonialism. The Social Worker. (49), 63-88.

Johnston, Charles M. (1964). The Valley of the Six Nations: A Collection of Documents on the Indian Lands of the Grand River. University of Toronto Press.

Johnston, Patrick. (1981). "Indigenous Children at Risk". Policy Options. (Nov.-Dec. 1981), 47-50.

Johnston, Patrick. (1983). Native Children and the Child Welfare System. James Lorimer and the Canadian Council on Social Development.

Johnston, Patrick. (2016). "Revisiting the "Sixties Scoop" of Indigenous children" (Policy Options, July 26, 2016) https://policyoptions.irpp.org/magazines/july-2016/revisiting-the-sixties-scoop-of-indigenous-children/

Long, John S. (2010). Treaty No. 9: Making the agreement to share the land in far northern Ontario in 1905. McGill-Queen's Press.

Lytwyn, Victor P. (2002). Mukekowuck Athinuwick: Original People of the Great Swampy Land. Winnipeg: University of Manitoba Press.

Mancini, Joe, and Stephanie Mancini. (2015). Transition to Common Work. Waterloo: Wilfrid Laurier University Press.

Manore, Jean L. (1993-4). "A Vision of Trust: The Legal, Moral, and Spiritual Foundations of Shingwauk Hall." Native Studies Review (9/2), 1-21.

Maté, Gabor. (2008). In the Realm of Hungry Ghosts: Close Encounters with Addiction. Knopf.

McLeod, William E. (2004). The Chapleau Game Preserve: History, Murder, and Other Tales. Betty Printing.

Noble, William C. (2015). "The Neutral Confederacy." The Canadian Encyclopedia. https://www.thecanadianencyclopedia.ca/en/article/neutral.

National Indian Brotherhood. (1972). Indian Control of Indian Education: Policy paper presented to the Minister of Indian Affairs and Northern Development. Retrieved from http://web.uvic.ca/ablo/documents/IndianControlofIndianEducation.pdf.

Paradis, Ryan. n.d. The Sixties Scoop A Literary Review prepared by the Manitoba Association of Friendship Centres. Winnipeg. http://www.friendshipcentres.ca/wp-content/uploads/2018/01/The-Sixties-Scoop-Literature-Review.pdf

Play, Fair. (1891). "The Future of Our Indians." The Canadian Indian. (1, March-June), 6-9.

Schreyer, Christine. (2003). "Travel Routes of the Chapleau Cree: An Ethnological Study." Algonquin Paper-Archive (34), 321-332.

Scott, Duncan C. et al. (1964) The James Bay Treaty: Treaty Number Nine. Queen's Printer. https://www.rcaanc-cirnac.gc.ca/eng/1100100028863/1581293189896

Shingwauk, Augustine. (1872). Little Pine's Journal: The Appeal of a Christian Chippeway Chief on Behalf of His People. Copp, Clark.

Simpson, Leanne. (2008). "Looking after Gdoo-naaganinaa: Precolonial Nishnaabeg Diplomatic and Treaty Relationships." Wicazo Sa Review (23/2, Fall), 29-42. 30131260.

Steiner, Sam. (2015). In Search of Promised Lands. Herald Press.

The Truth and Reconciliation Commission of Canada. (2015). Honouring the Truth, Reconciling for the Future: Summary of the Final Report of the Truth and Reconciliation Commission of Canada (Volume 1). James Lorimer & Co. Ltd.

Truth and Reconciliation Commission of Canada. (2015). Canada's Residential Schools: Missing Children and Unmarked Burials (Volume 4).

Truth and Reconciliation Commission of Canada. (2015). Canada's Residential Schools: The Legacy, The Final Report of the Truth and Reconciliation Commission of Canada (Volume 5).

Tuck, Eve. (2009). "Suspending Damage: A Letter to Communities." Harvard Educational Review (79/3, September), 409-428.

Younging, Gregory. (2018). Elements of Indigenous Style: A Guide for Writing by and about Indigenous Peoples. Brush Education, Inc.

ABOUT THE CO-AUTHORS

 Clarence Cachagee originates from Chapleau Cree First Nation and calls the Waterloo Region his home. He has an undeniable spirit for change. With a primary focus on working with the Spirit within, he is a helper, visionary and author who is known for investing his whole self into his community. Clarence has worked for a variety social service organizations in the field of homelessness, supportive housing, and education, with a focus on supporting Indigenous communities. Most recently, Clarence initiated Crow Shield Lodge, a non-profit Indigenous organization, serving as the Executive Director, focusing on land-based healing and teaching for all nations.

 Seth Ratzlaff is an emerging writer based in Kitchener, Ontario. He was born in the Niagara Region to Mennonite parents. Seth holds an undergraduate degree in English Rhetoric and a Master of Peace and Conflict Studies degree, both from the University of Waterloo. With a passion for storytelling and local history, he has been involved in a variety of grassroots initiatives, often focused on writing and the arts. Seth has experience in the fields of education and social support. He is now self-employed.